CHURCH DISCIPLINE AND THE COURTS

CHURCH DISCIPLINE AND THE COURTS

LYNN R. BUZZARD
AND
THOMAS S. BRANDON, JR.

Tyndale House Publishers, Inc.
Wheaton, Illinois

Unless otherwise indicated, all
Scripture is taken from *The Holy
Bible*, King James Version.

Cover photograph by Jim Steere

First printing, January 1987

Library of Congress Catalog Card Number 86-51191
ISBN 0-8423-0272-7
© 1986 by Lynn R. Buzzard and Thomas S. Brandon, Jr.
Printed in the United States of America

*Nothing could be more cruel than the
tenderness that consigns another to his sin.
Nothing could be more compassionate than
the severe rebuke that calls a brother back
from the path of sin.*

Dietrich Bonhoeffer, *Life Together*

*Every believer in Jesus Christ has the right to
be disciplined.*

Jay Adams, *More Than Redemption*

CONTENTS

1

PRIVATE AFFAIRS

It has all the marks of an upcoming Hollywood thriller—even an epic. In fact, rumors are that a movie may be forthcoming to the Bijou portraying the saga of Marian Guinn and the dour folks at the Collinsville Church of Christ in Oklahoma.

It ought to be a winner! It has all the right ingredients: sex, religion, and law rolled up into a tense drama of authority and power in a dusty town. Here is raw defiance and a nagging church. The plot pits the social outcast against entrenched power, hypocrisy, and self-righteousness. Hawthorne's *Scarlet Letter* and Hester Prynne have nothing on this tale. It will undoubtedly be R-rated—"for mature audiences only."

But it's all true! No need for the novelist to skillfully shape the mythical characters. These are real people! Many are familiar by now with the basic story. Marian Guinn had long been a member of the Church of Christ of Collinsville, Oklahoma, a small town of 2,200. Marian was more than a casual member. They knew her well. Several people in the 125-member church, including one of the defendants, Mr. Witten, had assisted her in moving to Collinsville with her children. Witten had baptized her. The church assisted her over an extended period of time, giving her a car on one occasion, setting up an account for gasoline, and providing baby-sitters while she studied for her GED. When she completed her GED the church threw a party for her and did the same a few years later when she graduated from Tulsa Junior College.

In 1980, church leaders, including the three elders whom she later sued, heard reports that she was having an affair with then town mayor Pat Sharp and confronted her. In Collinsville secrets were hard to keep, and even Marian admitted that there were "rumors" about town concerning her and Sharp. Sharp's former wife accused Marian of being partly to blame for the breakup of their marriage.

In the summer of 1981, when they heard further reports of an ongoing affair, they insisted she meet with them, praying with her and urging her to break off the relationship. According to court documents, at one point even Pat was tired of Marian and asked the church to help keep Marian from bothering him and his new girlfriend. But apparently Pat and Marian patched things up and the affair continued. Finally, after a stormy confrontation, church leaders warned her in a letter of September 21, 1981, that unless she publicly repented they would follow the mandate of Matthew 18 and "tell it to the church":

Dear Sister Marian,
It is with tremendous concern for your soul and the welfare of the Lord's church that we exhort you to consider the impact of the results of the course you have elected to pursue. We have and will continue to follow the instructions set forth

in the Scriptures in dealing with matters of church discipline. The Lord set forth the procedure in Matthew 18:15-17. We have confronted you personally . . . , however, to date you have not responded, so you leave us no alternative but to "tell it to the church." . . . It is the prayerful desire of the entire body of Christ that you correct this serious matter and avert the "withdrawing of fellowship" of the saints.

Marian didn't deny the allegations but declared it was "none of their business," and on September 24 wrote to the church and used the old "You can't fire me, I quit" approach:

I do not want my name mentioned before the church except to tell them I withdraw my membership immediately! I have never accepted your doctrine and never will. Anything I told was in confidence and not meant for anyone else to hear. You have no right to get up and say anything against me in church. . . . I have no choice but to attend another church, another denomination! Where men do not set themselves up as judges for God. He does his own judging.

The church proceeded, however, and on September 27 read to the members of the congregation a letter asking members to contact Marian about the "condition of her soul" and giving her until October 4 to repent. On October 5, and in a subsequent letter to the members, the church noted Scriptures they believed Marian had violated, removed her name from the rolls, and called on members to "continue to pray on her behalf and to contact her for purposes of encouragement and exhortation." The letter was then forwarded to Churches of Christ in Oolahah, Skiatook, Ramona, and Owasso—four sister congregations in the immediate geographical area with which they had a close relationship through members and financial support.

Following the American tradition, Miss
Guinn filed suit.[1] She sued the church itself
and its three elders, Ron Witten, Allan Cash,
and Ted Moody. The initial action was for
defamation, but her complaint was later
amended, dropping the action for defamation and claiming that the church's "public"
discipline and dismissal of her was an "invasion of privacy" and that these revelations
were "highly offensive and of no legitimate
interest" to those informed. All of this, she
alleged, "permanently injured and damaged
. . . her good name and reputation." Furthermore, she claimed, the "extreme and outrageous conduct" of the defendants
"recklessly caused severe emotional distress." The amended complaint concluded
that the "defendants should be punished
therefore and made an example to others."

Miss Guinn told the court, "What I do or
do not do is between God and myself," and
alleged that the elders had no right to "mess
with someone else's life." Her attorney,
Thomas Fraser, certainly seemed to agree.
At the trial, Fraser told the jury in closing arguments: "I demand the right, on behalf of
Marian Guinn, to lead her life the way she
chooses." In what was surely more of a social and moral commentary than a legal one
Fraser added: "He was a single man. She
was a single lady. And this is America!"

The Oklahoma jury apparently agreed and
awarded her $205,000 actual damages, add-
ing another $185,000 punitive damages.
Some jurors reportedly wanted an even higher award.

The church seemed undaunted by the
opinions of the Oklahoma jurors. Its leaders
had clearly stated from the beginning that
their practices of church discipline were
rooted in biblical convictions set forth in
Matthew 18, and that they had a duty as el-

ders to "admonish, encourage, and counsel" members of the congregation. The issue was sharply drawn now, and Elder Ron Witten put it directly: "Any time God's law conflicts with man's law, we have to stick with God's law."

The press soon descended on the town and its hot news. It unsurprisingly pictured the church as oppressive and intrusive. It was a "quotable" time in Collinsville. Marian characterized the church's call for her to repent or be censured as "blackmail." Attorney Fraser depicted the elders as a "squad" that would go around and "enforce the edicts of the church." Letters to local newspapers expressed a similar tone. One person wrote the following:

I cannot believe four Church of Christ officials . . . have anointed themselves and set about to pass judgment on one of their members. . . . Taking up worship time to slander and belittle a person in front of a Sunday congregation is worthy of discipline itself.

Another citizen stated:

How a person lives his private life is between that person and God, not between that person and the elders of the church. Let these elders tend to more critical matters of their church.

MARIAN'S PROGENY

It was a pot of gold at the end of the rainbow. Even before the case finally had been reviewed by the appellate courts, similar cases were filed across the country. In California, often the home of new causes of legal action, the Christian Community Church, its pastor, Ernest Gentile, and its board of elders were sued by John R. Kelly.[2] Kelly alleged that Elder Donald Phillips, a family counselor who undertook to counsel the plaintiff, "disclosed confidential, intimate, and embarrassing details of his sexual and marital life" and that the church "publicly released" this information and "publicly excommunicated him in church services on April 24, 1983." He claimed that such action was professional malpractice, a breach of fiduciary duty, and, as in the *Guinn* case, "outrageous conduct" resulting in emotional distress. Kelly also added counts of reckless and careless negligence, invasion of privacy, and even one for conspiracy. In keeping with the broad scope of the complaint he asked for a judgment of actual damages plus $5 million for "exemplary and punitive damages."

In Orange County, California, a more modest plaintiff, Jan Brown, asked for $3 million against officials of the Fairview Church of Christ in Garden Grove for publicly denouncing her divorce as "sinful behavior."[3] The complaint alleged that Pastor Ken Dart read a letter on January 22, 1984, saying that "for so long as she refuses to repent, none of us should keep company or associate with her in any way that would suggest approval of these actions. . . ." The church leaders read Scriptures in connection with the discipline; Brown claimed these accused her of adultery. Dart and six elders were sued. The court summonses were served on the elders at the church on Easter Sunday.

On Sunday, October 14, 1984, another group of church leaders were served legal papers in a suit by James Shive and other family members.[4] Pastor Grant Adkisson, other staff, and the deacons of the First Baptist Church of Pagosa Springs, a Southern Baptist congregation in Denver, were the targets. The complaint didn't mince any words, alleging that on September 11, 1983, the defendants slandered the plaintiff, James

▶14

Shive, before the congregation, publicly ac-
cusing him of being a "heretic, deceiver,
fornicator, coveter, idolater, liar, [and] disorderly," among other attributes. Other counts
in the complaint alleged libel, invasions of
privacy, and infliction of emotional distress
by outrageous conduct in "wanton and reckless disregard" of the plaintiffs. Each of sev-
enteen claims sought damages of $1 million.
Not content with monetary recovery, Shive
and others in a separate but related legal
action sought reinstatement of their membership, an injunction against any church interference with their rights, and a court
order requiring the defendants to turn over
the church property to them [5]

In Santa Cruz on October 14, 1984, Charles
R. Roberson sued the Evangelical Orthodox
Church, ten named church leaders, and, to
make sure he didn't miss anyone, five hun-
dred "John Does" in connection with an alleged public revelation of a "confidential"
confession of marital infidelity by the plaintiff, a former bishop of the Evangelical
Orthodox Church.[6] The complaint is a shopping list of tort claims: invasion of privacy,
breach of fiduciary duty, false imprisonment,
emotional distress, conspiracy, interference
with prospective economic advantage, and
other charges. To set things straight, Roberson asked the court for $5 million in general
damages and another $5 million in punitive
damages.

In Philadelphia, Devere Ganges asked for
$1 million in damages against the New Cen-
tral Baptist Church for libel and slander in
excommunicating him. He alleged that Rev.
Leonard M. Howard defamed him in calling
him a "heathen." Ganges's attorney insists
Ganges is not a heathen and is seeking reinstatement of his membership and the right
to communion.

Many Christians on hearing the news from the Sooners were unsympathetic with the Collinsville Church, citing their harshness and lack of forgiveness. Even conservative voices expressed reservations. Some didn't like the idea of discipline, others thought it ought to be private. Still others insisted it was over when Marian quit. *The Baptist Messenger* (Oklahoma), a Southern Baptist publication, noted in an editorial a series of "errors" the church had committed, including public reading of the letter of dismissal and sending it to sister churches. A lawsuit, they observed, could have been avoided if the church "had allowed the woman to leave the church membership quietly." The public condemnation was "slander," the *Baptist Messenger* reported, inaccurately, since slander was not even an allegation. A careful reading of the facts, however, suggests the church was acting quite consistently not only with its own doctrinal commitments, but even within a strong Christian tradition. It may have been out of touch with contemporary styles, but the issues run deeper.

Church discipline is always a touchy subject, mixing as it does matters of judgment and forgiveness, individual liberty and community values. And surely over the years enough harm has been done in the name of church discipline to give all of us some pause. But should we, therefore, abandon it? Was Marian Guinn's attorney right when he bluntly put it into sharp relief: "It doesn't matter if she was fornicating up and down the street. It doesn't give [the church] the right to stick their noses in it"?

Is church discipline a relic of a Pharisaic frontier religion mired in Victorian morality and judgmental self-righteousness? Or is it the necessary and proper response of a reli-

VICTIM OR JUST DESERTS?

gious community with moral values committed to the biblical call to holiness?

MIND YOUR OWN BUSINESS!

Minding your own business, though hardly biblical law, has become a popular guide to limiting snoops and busybodies. But whose business is the "private" immorality of a church member? Is it any of the church's business? And what of Caesar and the courts? Ought courts to discipline churches who discipline their members? Are the courts about to force churches out of the discipline business? Can churches no longer pass moral judgments or expel members? Can the Amish "shun" an errant brother? Do people have a "right" to privacy from their fellow church members? from criticism? Can a church expel members but be legally required to be tight-lipped about why? And what about those high-sounding protections of religious liberty, free exercise, rights of association, and free speech? *Whose business is church discipline, anyway?*

The issue is far broader than rural Oklahoma fundamentalist churches. It goes deeper than local church autonomy. Roman Catholic discipline issues have emerged with increasing frequency in recent years, especially in the light of what the controversial priest Andrew Greely has called the emergence of the "do-it-yourself Catholic." Should courts interfere if the Roman Catholic Church follows through on its threat to expel the twenty-four Catholic sisters who signed a full-page ad in the *New York Times* in October 1984 suggesting that "a diversity of opinions regarding abortion exist among committed Catholics"? Archbishop John May of St. Louis called the action of the sisters a "scandal, . . . a flagrant, flashy, and deliberate affront." Maureen Reiff, one of the signers, disagreed: "This is a pivotal moment in the history of the church. . . . We all feel that the attack on us appears to be a rescinding of Vatican II." A Vatican official, however, declared: "The issue is simple . . . either [the sisters] accept the church's teaching or they don't. Either they are in or they are out."[7]

Swiss theologian Hans Kung, himself subject to discipline, complained that "a new phase of Inquisition" has begun. Notre Dame theologian Richard McBrien, chairman of the theology department, queried, "Are we back to book burnings, blacklistings, expulsion, and even excommunications?"[8]

The *Guinn* case has brought all these tensions to the surface and a new interest is emerging in the whole issue of church discipline. Recent books, such as Don Baker's sensitive story of the discipline of a church staff member, have suggested that discipline can, even must, make a comeback.[9] In fact, for Baker such discipline is not optional but "mandatory." Christian magazines have also dealt with this issue. For example, stories have appeared in *Leadership, Moody Monthly,* and *Eternity.*[10]

A national conference was held in New Mexico on the issue of current church discipline under the theme "Restoring the Ministry of Discipline to the Church." Conference speakers called for a return to a biblically faithful model of discipline.

The issues are complex and emotional. Noted theologian Martin Marty declared in response to the intervention of the Oklahoma courts, "This is going to get mighty sticky. There's no telling where it is going to go."[11] For Forrest Montgomery of the National Association of Evangelicals, the issue is central: "What's at stake is the church's very existence."[12] Observers all seem to agree with a judgment made about church discipline twenty-five years ago by Herbert Bouman: "This matter is no child's play."[13]

NOTES

[1]*Guinn v. Church of Christ of Collinsville,* No. 81-929 (Dist. Ct. Tulsa County, Okla., filed Nov. 23, 1981).

[2]*Kelly v. Christian Community Church,* No. 545117 (Super. Ct. Santa Clara County, Cal., filed March 22, 1984).

[3]*Brown v. Fairview Church of Christ,* No. 4277621 (Super. Ct. Orange County, Cal., filed April 20, 1984).

[4]*Shive v. Adkisson,* No. 84 CV 6646 (Denver County Ct., Colo., filed Sept. 6, 1983).

[5]*Ash v. First Baptist Church,* No. 83 CV 132 (Archuleta County Ct., Colo., filed Dec. 19, 1983).

[6]*Roberson v. Evangelical Orthodox Church,* No. 981129 (Super. Ct. Santa Cruz County, Cal., filed Oct. 15, 1984).

[7]"Women: Second-Class Citizens?" *Time,* 4 Feb. 1985, 62, 63.

[8]"Discord in the Church," *Time,* 4 Feb. 1985, 52, 53.

[9]Don Baker, *Beyond Forgiveness: The Healing Touch of Church Discipline* (Portland, Oreg.: Multnomah Press, 1984).

[10]See Paul Benware, "Mind Your Own Business," *Moody Monthly,* Jan 1984, 24-27; Ben Patterson, "Discipline: The Backbone of the Church," *Leadership,* Winter 1983, 108-113; Tom Stafford, "The Tightrope: A Case Study in Church Discipline," *Leadership,* Summer 1984, 40-48; Don Baker, "The High Cost of Church Discipline," *Eternity,* Sept. 1984, 29-31.

[11]Roberta Green, "Church Discipline: Can Courts Pass Judgment?" *The Register,* 29 Apr. 1984, A18, 19.

[12]Ibid.

[13]Herbert J. A. Bouman, "Biblical Presuppositions for Church Discipline," *Concordia Theological Monthly,* July 1959, 515.

2 MINDING THE CHURCH'S BUSINESS

"It was none of the church's business," declared Marian Guinn. Perhaps we can all join Marian and agree that the church ought to mind its own business. But what is the "business" of the church? Is discipline a legitimate business activity of the community of faith? Or should the church stick to "more important things" as the letters to the editor in the Collinsville newspaper suggested? What is the church about?

Certainly the secularist, like Marian, wants to see the church "stay in its place"—confined to what he perceives as a religious ghetto. It is to be nonintrusive, nonjudgmental: the church should offer solace, an escape from life "out there," even worship. But it ought not to forget its place—and certainly passing moral judgment is outside its competence, a dangerous excursion outside its territory.[1] Perhaps, as Marian's lawyer argued, a $390,000 judgment would teach the church to mind its own business next time!

As the Collinsville case vividly illustrates, we live in a day when the whole concept of discipline, accountability, judgment—even

▶21

guilt—is not simply passé but is perceived as unhealthy, if not dangerous. The spirit of our age is hostile to the very principles that underlie the biblical concepts of the church, including moral absolutes, spiritual accountability, and individual responsibility.

These attitudes are not just "out there": they have crept subtly into the church itself. The thrust of the *Guinn* case targets not so much the distortions of the courts as those of the church. In communicating on the *Guinn* decision, Sam Ericsson, executive director of the Christian Legal Society, declared he didn't blame the court as much as he did the church at large. The universal church has so seldom practiced biblical discipline that when a local congregation does so, it is perceived as so strange and bizarre that a jury can call it "outrageous."

What is "outrageous"? Something that grossly offends the values and standards of conduct of the society. There is irony and a wealth of commentary in the fact that no longer is it *Marian's* conduct, but the *church's* that "offends" the good folks of Collinsville. Clearly, in the minds of Collinsville judges and jurors, society's values are the premises for the whole rationale of perceiving church discipline as "outrageous."

The church that disciplines does indeed fly in the face of many of our most cherished social concepts—notions we believe have become distorted. What are some of these notions that result in church discipline being labeled "outrageous"?

Every man did what was right in his own eyes. *Judges 17:6, NASB*

INDIVIDUALISM

A "do it yourself" religion[2] is a direct product of the modern version of individualism, precisely the sort portrayed by Marian Guinn in her insistence that what she does is exclusively between her and God. Religion is perceived as a "private" matter, a sort of bilateral negotiable contract. Churches might gather these private contractors together, but certainly ought not to disturb their personal agreements with God. If religion is simply a private, individual question, then church discipline becomes an intrusion, indeed, an invasion of the sanctuary of the soul. But it was the great social historian R. H. Tawney who warned about the delusions of such a private religion: "The man who seeks God in isolation from his fellows is likely to find, not God, but the Devil, who will bear an embarrassing resemblance to himself."[3]

Such is the religious fallout of the sweeping, narcissistic individualism rampant in Western civilization today. Our whole society has become atomized, caught up in individual self-fulfillment. Christopher Lasch's *The Culture of Narcissism*[4] has laid bare the decadence that marks such a society; modern man's "protective shallowness, his avoidance of dependence, his inability to mourn."[5] This kind of pseudo-freedom that seeks faith outside any community produces, in fact, a kind of a bondage—the bondage of homelessness and a spiritual wandering masquerading as a holy pilgrimage.[6]

This quest for individualism promised a glorious autonomy. It is Maslow's "self-actualized, creative, and autonomous" man who is the modern adult. But something has gone wrong. "The satisfactions of individualism come at an incalculable price," Daniel Yankelovich warned.[7]

The cost to community, human relationships, and mutual commitments has been high. The "autonomy of personality" advocated by widely respected counseling theorists such as Rollo May and Carl Rogers has some unhappy side effects. "Limited liability" marks modern relationships, according to Alvin Toffler.[8] We have become "new nomads," free from commitments, searching for novelty and diversity in an age marked by transience. "Temporariness . . . increasingly characterizes human relations" leading inextricably to a "freedom without responsibility."[9]

As we look around us, at mid-twentieth century, [one] of the most distressing "symptoms" of our times [is a] confusion and apathy in the matter of moral values.
O. H. Mowrer, The Crisis in Psychiatry and Religion[10]

LOSS OF NORMS AND VALUES

It is not a long step from a radical individualism to the loss of those norms and values that would limit this autonomy. The logical progression is this: "If I am to be totally free, I must reject those bonds that constrain me and throw off the yoke of all oppressions. Norms, rules, and standards inhibit and restrain. My emancipation proclamation is indiscriminate and absolute."

And so goes Western civilization. In such a world the church's moral "absolutes" are mere opinions that bind only those who need such "crutches" for their consciences. Let each man and woman in the autonomy of their own consciences choose their own values. Let us simply encourage one another to "be true to ourselves."

If there are no more absolutes in a relativistic, evolutionary worldview, all we can possibly do is assist people to "clarify" their values—to choose values freely, prize them, and act on them.[11]

Thus, we have shifted to a purely subjective morality in which intention and motivation, rather than the content of a moral vision, are dispositive of its value.[12] We can inquire about sincerity and purpose but not truth! By this standard, the Collinsville church committed a grievous error: it assumed it knew something about values, something above the personal decisions and tastes of individuals.[13]

So, horror of horrors, let us not "impose" or "indoctrinate" such values. And we can surely expect our enlightened and modern churches to shun any temptations to moral assertiveness!

The problems with such an approach to values are more than merely personal moral tragedies, for which there is ample evidence around us. The consequences are social, for norms are a form of social glue without which nothing holds together and society cannot in fact exist. "Norms are what keep us from degenerating into that nightmare of solipsistic anarchy. . . ."[14] This is not merely a matter of the integrity of the church but of our culture and society. Can civilization exist in a meaningful sense, and can there be community—not merely geographic proximity—without a shared moral commitment, a shared vision that "calls" us beyond ourselves?[15]

LOSS OF AUTHORITY

The crucial issue of our age is one of authority, according to Hannah Arendt. That issue is a natural consequence of a distorted version of individualism combined with a loss of any reference point for established norms and values. Shall the modern, self-authenticating, liberated person look for truth? If so, where can he turn? And what of the modern, liberated, self-actualized, autonomous human being, the one envisioned by contemporary secular writers? Why surely he will not or dares not turn anywhere, for this man is, as Carl Rogers proudly hailed, "unblocked."

In such an ideological environment, concepts of church discipline will not flourish. Paul Witz effectively observed that the "selfism" that dominates contemporary psychology is "an ideology hostile to discipline and obedience."[16]

Indeed, the modern concept of adulthood has excluded the notion of accountability. We have been allured with the vision that adulthood is setting aside childlike obedience and accountability and "doing your own thing." A founder of Reba Place Fellowship in Evanston, Illinois, queried a local congregation, "Where in the world do young people get the notion that when you grow up you can do whatever you want?" The answer, he suggested, is that the idea comes from us all. The models our young people see are adult models of noncommunity, nonaccountability, individualism sliding into narcissism, privatism into loneliness, illusory freedom into rootlessness. We have "imaged" adulthood as being unbound. No wonder that when young people begin to think they are "adult" they claim the same liberty and autonomy. In such an environment notions of authority and moral absolutes are rejected.[17]

All of us are affected by the loss of structures and commitments to authority and accountability. It has happened in our families, in our communities, and even in our churches. The lesson we have learned from *Guinn* is that the church cannot successfully teach ideology her members have rejected.

At three I had a feeling of
    Ambivalence toward my brothers,
And so it follows naturally
    I poisoned all my lovers.

REJECTION OF GUILT

But now I'm happy; I have learned
  The lesson this has taught;
That everything I do that's wrong,
  Is someone else's fault.

Anna Russell, "Psychiatric Folksong"[18]

In an age without norms, in a culture that
has rejected absolutes, it is not surprising
that "guilt" is forbidden as a relic of a past
age, a disabling remnant of authoritarian interests. The only thing to feel guilty about is
guilt itself. And of course, without real guilt,
there can be no valid judgment, no need for
confession, repentance, or restoration. In one
fell swoop, a mass of Christian doctrine has
been declared heresy. Perhaps in no other
area does contemporary culture, particularly
the modern god of psychology, clash so
sharply with biblical thought.

We have been told that such concepts are
destructive of our fulfillment and contrary to
love. We may be "sick," but surely we have
not sinned! In the new lexicon, loaded words
such as *good* and *bad* have been replaced (I
suppose because they're not "good") with
mature and *immature, productive* and *unpro-
ductive,* or *socially adjusted* and *socially
maladjusted.*[19]

We live today with an enormous cultural
bias against "judgment." Guilt and judgment
are the deadly sins of modern man. In religion and pop psychology alike the motto is
love and self-acceptance. We have been
"saturated and marinated in love without
content," Bob Mumford warns.

The role of the church in dealing with
what it used to call "sin" and evil, naming it
and offering release and renewal, has been
challenged by new thoughts and new institutions. Karl Menninger noted unhappily
that the "major responsibility for identifying
and dealing with adult misbehavior has been

taken over by the state."[20] The foremost crit-
ic of the co-opting of the church by secularist
institutions and ideology has been Mowrer.
He decries the "secularization" of the "management of the problem of guilt" and observes that, whereas such problems were
once largely in the hands of the church, "the
fact is that those persons most deeply burdened and broken by guilt and moral failure
are now quite regularly turned over by the
churches to the state," whose agencies such
as mental hospitals are a "failure." It is time,
he implores, to rethink the whole concept of
helping "guilt-ridden persons in a secular,
medically controlled setting."[21] These concepts rejecting major biblical themes have
dominated not only secular circles but even
the church. Modern pastoral care emphases,
although commendable, have all too often
uncritically adopted the secular perspectives
of contemporary psychiatry and psychology,
and Freudian or other secular schools of
thought. Mowrer sadly notes that the church
has sold its birthright for a mess of porridge:

What more eloquent testimony could one ask of
the loss of authority and confidence on the part of
the clergy than the tendency to regard secular
healers as the "professionals" in this area. If, as
we now increasingly suspect, moral issues are nu-
clear to every neurosis, isn't it remarkable that
the clergy no longer regards itself as first in competence here.[22]

One psychiatrist even complimented a
group of fundamentalist ministers for being
"fifty years behind the times in psychology"
because it had spared them a "long Freudian
detour."[23]

Fortunately, there is an increasing recognition today in some professional counseling
circles of the significance of great biblical
themes such as guilt, conscience, confession,
and sin.

GUILT IS REAL AND HEALTHY.

Blessed is he whose transgression is forgiven,
*   whose sin is covered.*
When I kept silence,
*   my bones waxed old through my roaring all*
*   the day long.*
I acknowledged my sin unto thee,
*   and mine iniquity have I not hid.*
I said, I will confess my transgressions unto the
*   Lord;*
*   and thou forgavest the iniquity of my sin.*
Psalm 32:1, 3, 5

The idea of sin is making a comeback.
Time[24]

There is a fundamental assertion about the character of guilt and the power of confession in this psalm. It is an invitation to give up the futility of hypocrisy and self-illusion, recognize the reality of our guilt, and open ourselves to the liberation of confession and power of forgiveness. This profoundly biblical insight, though rejected by much of modern psychology, is gaining credibility among therapists.

William Glasser's "reality therapy" and other secular theories are built on the notion of personal responsibility, emphasizing the actual *moral issues* in behavior.[25] Belgum described the symptoms of those seeking therapy as "the amplified and distorted voice of conscience," and the appropriate response for one so stricken as "penitence in the face of guilt, rather than a plea of irresponsible illness."[26]

Karl Menninger went even further and used the forbidden word *sin*. Sin is a "proud word," he insisted. Although behavioral theorists eschew the concept of personal moral responsibility, Menninger said of sin, "The reality it signifies is energetic and destructive" and "haunts our age as much as any, perhaps more so."[27]

Some secular theorists are beginning to recognize that a proper concept of sin—of fault—is actually liberating. It allows one to identify the wrong, confess, and be done with it, and not be trapped by mechanistic behavioral and Freudian models. The idea that we ought not to condemn ourselves is *not* self-respect, suggests Mowrer. "Who wants to lose his capacity to condemn and punish himself if he really behaves badly? This is surely the Pearl of Great Price."[28]

CONFESSION IS NECESSARY AND LIBERATING.

Suppressed sin, like suppressed steam, is dangerous. Confession is the safety valve.
Leslie Weatherhead[29]

He who is alone with his sin is utterly alone.
Dietrich Bonhoeffer[30]

The dangers of repressed guilt are well known: anger, illness, resentment, withdrawal. The solution is not to ignore the warning lamp of guilt, or unscrew it, happily alleging a defective signal, but to correct the problem by confession. Only then can the dynamic of forgiveness provide release, and such forgiveness is at the heart of confession and church discipline. But the power of confession is more than a personal act of release and restoration. It is, Bonhoeffer wrote, "the breakthrough to community."

Sin demands to have a man by himself. It withdraws him from community. The more isolated a person is, the more destructive will be the power of sin over him, and the more deeply he becomes involved in it, the more disastrous is his isolation. Sin wants to remain unknown. It shuns the light. . . . In confession the light of the gospel breaks into the darkness and seclusion of the heart. The sin must be brought into the light. The unexpressed must be openly spoken and acknowledged. All that is secret and hidden is made manifest. It is a hard struggle until the sin is openly admitted.[31]

Don Baker writes movingly of the emotional release of confession for Greg, a pastor who had hidden adulterous affairs throughout his ministry. Greg had been miserable, "looking over his shoulder" for thirteen years—until finally the truth was out.[32] Now, for the first time, healing was a possibility. Freedom was now, and only now, possible.

CONFRONTATION IS POWERFUL AND HEALING. Nothing is less popular than "judging." One might suspect it is the new unforgivable sin. It conjures up spectres of snoops and arrogant, self-righteous persons. Biblical images of logs and motes pass before our minds, and we are reminded of the passage "Judge not, that ye be not judged" (Matt. 7:2).

Contemporary pastoral counseling has tended to reject any notion of spiritual counsel as involving judgment. Noted pastoral counseling author Seward Hiltner rejects judgment in the "shepherding" work of pastors. In the 1950s, Carl Rogers's "nondirective" and "client-centered" counseling had little room for external and supposedly arbitrary judgment.

But perhaps we have dismissed the question too abruptly, failing to distinguish the nature and scope of a proper biblical judgment from that kind condemned by our Lord.

Confrontation, judgment, and truth-telling may indeed be the basis of effective and loving relationships. Confrontation by others may be the powerful invitation to wholeness we all so desperately seek. It is a refusal to let others live alone in their pain and guilt. Life without such confrontation is directionless, and confrontation is often a gift to jolt us out of mediocrity.[33]

The noted Swiss doctor, Paul Tournier, calls them "acts of honesty." While rejecting a "judgmental spirit," he speaks of the importance of an "exchange [of] accumulated grievances" as the necessary precondition of real peace, mutual forgiveness and the "rebirth of reciprocal confidence."[34]

We are unaccustomed to such "exchanges," preferring instead our silent resentments. We have persuaded ourselves that kindness to others is avoiding the truth. "What was really bugging me was the fact that for the first time in my life an adult had let me have it straight," noted Bill Milliken in recounting how shocked he was when as a youth he was corrected and "judged" by a staff camp leader.[35] Yet Milliken insisted it was an act that began to set him free.

CONCLUSION

The church must mind its business. The tragedy today is twofold. First, we in the church have forgotten what our business is, the breadth of its scope, and the depth of its earnestness. Second, perhaps arising from the first tragedy, is that the concept of "church" so prevalent in our culture is increasingly out of touch with biblical understandings. It is a quasi-church. At times it is a co-opted church whose patterns of thought are shaped by culture rather than by biblical perspectives. To the extent that this is so, we are threatened with being a worldly church. Harry Blamires, an English literature professor, accurately perceived the danger that while the church may have a Christian ethic and a Christian liturgy it does not have a Christian mind.[36] Our mind has been captured by the world.

In such an environment, there is enormous

potential for surprise when the church takes a strong stand on an issue. Our first task is surely, like our Lord's, to be certain we are about our Father's business!

NOTES

[1]Spirituality in such a view is, unlike the biblical tradition or any "ethical" religion, divorced from ethics and morality—either public or private. Spirituality becomes more Eastern in flavor, a state of being, even an escape from the rigors of human existence.

[2]Ben Patterson, "Discipline: The Backbone of the Church," *Leadership,* Winter 1983, 110.

[3]Ibid., 111.

[4]Christopher Lasch, *The Culture of Narcissism* (New York: Norton, 1979).

[5]Ibid., 50.

[6]Cornelius J. Dyck, "Early Ideas of Authority," in *Studies in Church Discipline,* ed. Maynard Shelley (Newton, Kans.: Faith & Life, 1958), 38.

[7]Ibid., 121.

[8]Alvin Toffler, *Future Shock* (New York: Random House, 1970), 97.

[9]Ibid., 96.

[10]O. H. Mowrer, *The Crisis in Psychiatry and Religion* (Princeton, N.J.: D. Van Nostrand Co., 1961), 58.

[11]See, for example, Sidney B. Simon, L. Howe, and H. Kirshenbaun, *Values Clarification* (New York: Dodd, Mead, & Co., 1985). Simon's work is widely used in education and is commendable despite considerable criticism from Christian groups. Students need to learn to choose, prize, and act upon values. Questions have legitimately been raised about whether or not utilizing typical values clarification exercises with young children tends to promote the concept that values are merely what we choose without any reference point. However, when a society has no common value commitments, all that is left for education is mere "clarification." We can't teach any substantive values because we don't know what they are. We can only describe our own. It is, thus, a sign of the loss of shared values.

[12]Thomas P. Sweetser, "What Ever Happened to Confession," in *New Catholic World,* Jan./Feb. 1984, 31, 32.

[13]It is worth noting that today people are inclined to criticize anyone "imposing" values on others, or even talking as if his values were "right"; yet in other areas our society individually, collectively, and freely asserts moral postures and roundly condemns those whose conduct does not conform—e.g., in areas such as anti-discrimination law, human rights, racial justice, economic justice, anti-semitism, etc. That is, in some arenas we increasingly recognize that "moral" notions are not totally elective, yet in other arenas we want people to act as if moral judgments are purely personal. Some seek to differentiate these two situations by insisting that one area reflects questions of "public" interest or relevance as opposed to purely "personal" morality. But such a distinction often merely begs the question as to what conduct has public consequences and is of legitimate interest to society.

[14]Daniel Yankelovich, New Rules (New York: Random House, 1981), 86.

[15]The problem actually goes beyond the West. Commentators on developments in China have noted that communism destroyed the Confucian basis for moral principles that provided the basis for its civilization. Now that the cultural revolution and its radical communism have been rejected, the communist ideological basis for its culture is equally devastated. What is left on which to build a community? The same has been suggested for Russia and its European satellites; that is, no one really believes communism any more, so on what shall the state, much less the civilization, be grounded? Little is left in such environments except power, status, and consumption!

[16]Paul Vitz, Psychology As Religion (Grand Rapids: Eerdmans, 1977), 62.

[17]Charles Reich in his Greening of America (New York: Random House, 1970), noted that the surge of individualism in what he terms "consciousness III" would deeply threaten norms and authorities. Daniel Yankelovich speaks of the "flabby and self-centered morality" that emerges from the modern preoccupation with the self and the resulting anomie that arises from the disunity and disarray of collapsing norms (New Rules, 171).

[18]Cited by Mowrer, 49.

[19]So suggests noted sociologist of Middletown fame, Helen M. Lynd, On Shame and the Search for Identity (New York: Harcourt Brace & Co., 1958), 18.

[20]Karl Menninger, Whatever Became of Sin? (New York: Hawthorn Books, 1973), 24.

[21]Mowrer, 167.

[22]Mowrer, 197. Leo Steines, speaking in 1958 at Harvard, declared: "The ministry makes a tremendous mistake when it swaps what it has for psychoanalytic dressing." Cited by Jay Adams, *Competent to Counsel* (Grand Rapids, Mich.: Baker, 1970), 18. The *Nally v. Grace Community Church* "clergy malpractice" case deals precisely with this issue. The plaintiff alleged that the church and its clergy were negligent in failing "to refer" the troubled young Nally to secular counselors. The legal theory is that there is a "duty to refer" and the church breached that duty. See Samuel E. Ericsson, *Clergy Malpractice: Legal and Policy Issues* (Oak Park, Ill.: Christian Legal Society, 1982).

[23]Cited by David Belgum, *Guilt: Where Religion and Psychology Meet* (Englewood Cliffs, N.J.: Prentice Hall, 1963), 93.

[24]"Sin and Psychology," *Time,* 14 Sept. 1959, 69.

[25]William Glasser, *Reality Therapy* (New York: Harper & Row, 1975).

[26]Belgum, *Guilt,* 54.

[27]Menninger, *Sin,* 40. Citing Bernard Murchland with approval, Mowrer similarly suggests that once one introduces the idea of moral judgment, one "might as well beard the lion and use the strongest term of all, sin" (*Crisis in Psychiatry,* 40).

[28]Mowrer, 163.

[29]Cited by Mowrer, 213.

[30]Dietrich Bonhoeffer, *Life Together* (New York: Harper & Row, 1976), 112.

[31]Ibid., 112.

[32]Don Baker, *Beyond Forgiveness: The Healing Touch of Church Discipline* (Portland, Oreg.: Multnomah Press, 1984), 81.

[33]David Augsburger, *Caring Enough to Confront* (Glendale, Calif.: Regal Books, 1980), 51.

[34]Paul Tournier, *Guilt and Grace* (New York: Harper & Row, 1958), 80.

[35]Bill Milliken, *Tough Love* (Old Tappan, N.J.: Revell, 1968), 14.

[36]Harry Blamires, *The Christian Mind* (Ann Arbor, Mich.: Servant Books, 1981).

3 NO DISCIPLINE, NO CHURCH

Church discipline did not begin with the sessions of the elders at Collinsville, nor did the arguments about it begin with the lawyers in *Guinn*. Church discipline has a long if controversial history.

DISCIPLINE IN THE OLD TESTAMENT

The Old Testament contains the antecedents if not the origins of church discipline. "Ye shall be holy, for I the Lord your God am holy" (Lev. 19:2) sets the stage for the expectations of a holy God of chosen people. This principle of God's holiness in both its ethical and transcendent dimensions is a "biblical presupposition" for church discipline.[1]

God's holiness works itself out in a number of other Old Testament themes with implications for church discipline. This holy God brooks no competitors, unmistakably rejecting idolatry: "Thou shalt have no other gods before me" (Exod. 30:3). His holiness abhors evil and excludes the presence of the unholy: Adam and Eve are banished and Moses is prohibited from entering the Promised Land. And this holy God enters into a covenant with a people who are to be holy, a sanctified nation chartered and ruled by

God. This people are set apart and separated for they are uniquely his.[2]

These covenant people and God made vows, solemn, irrevocable pledges of loyalty: "I will be their God and they will be my people." Keeping this covenant is at the heart of Old Testament thought, and to breach a covenant is an act sure to bring about serious consequences. This God who calls and covenants is a chastising, disciplining Lord who exercises judgment, justice, and righteousness throughout the earth.

These convictions are the basis for discipline in the Old Testament. The most frequently cited account is the "sin in the camp" at Ai and the judgment on Achan found in Joshua 7. Other accounts of discipline include the discipline of Israel over the golden calf (Exod. 32:19-29, 35) and for the breaking of vows (Lev. 26:14-46; Deut. 17:2-7; 29:25-28, 31:16-17; Judg. 2:20-23). Punishment varied from death (Exod. 22:20) to forfeiture of property (Ezra 9:2-10:8).[3]

Community discipline was further developed by the Jewish community during the diaspora, and the Talmud provides multiple levels of community censure including short-term and full excommunication.[4]

DISCIPLINE IN THE NEW TESTAMENT

"Sin and discipline appear in the very earliest period of the church."[5] Jesus himself faced the issue of sin and failure among his disciples with Judas and Peter.

The New Testament shares Old Testament convictions about the holiness of God and his nonnegotiable demands, although it is clear that certain New Testament teachings modified the harshness of Jewish legalism prevalent in the first century.[6] The New Testament gives us a picture of a community that very early practiced discipline.

BASIC DOCTRINES. As with the Old Testament, the New Testament practice of church discipline is rooted in basic doctrines. The holiness of God and his expectations of a holy people are consistent with Old Testament teachings (1 Pet. 2:5, 9; Eph. 5:25-27). We are his temple and called to sanctification (1 Thess. 4:3; Rom. 12:1-2, 6:19; 1 Pet. 1:15) and to perfection (Matt. 5:48). Consider the central confession of the New Testament: Jesus is Lord! The very notion of Lord evinces a claim of obedience that brooks no diminution. Lordship assumes discipline, obedience, and correction.

One might look also to other basic New Testament themes such as confession, repentance, judgment, the kingdom, diakonia, and koinonia to draw inferences for church discipline.

SPECIFIC TEACHINGS. Church discipline does not rest merely on the permutations of basic doctrine, but emerges from specific New Testament instruction and examples. The key passage, the "divine warrant"[7] for church discipline is Matthew 18:15-18.

Moreover, if thy brother shall trespass against thee, go and tell him his fault between thee and him alone: if he shall hear thee, thou hast gained thy brother. But if he will not hear thee, then take with thee one or two more, that in the mouth of two or three witnesses every word may be established. And if he shall neglect to hear them, tell it unto the church: but if he neglect to hear the church, let him be unto thee as a heathen man and a publican. I say unto you, Whatsoever ye shall bind on earth shall be bound in heaven: and whatsoever ye shall loose on earth shall be loosed in heaven.

Here is specific instruction from our Lord regarding the church's commitment to and procedures for church discipline. Here there is no indifference as to sin; rather "should ever any one of them go astray, there must be an all-out, concerted, determined, inexorable effort at recovery," even to the point of the "shock treatment of expulsion."[8] The entire process calls upon all the resources of the community to seek reconciliation and restoration, increasing the level of engagement and breadth of involvement at each step. It is not a casual discipline of expulsion of the unwanted or erring but a commitment of the family to one of its members. Only when that member repeatedly and insistently rejects the community is he granted the freedom that he wishes.

The other portions of Matthew 18 reinforce this: God seeks the one lost sheep and rejoices when it is found (vv. 12, 13), the Father is unwilling that any of the little ones be lost (v. 14), his forgiveness reaches seventy times seven (v. 22), and we have a duty to forgive as we have been forgiven lest judgment fall upon us (vv. 23-35).

Here also in verses 18-20 are the authority and power of the church, the keys of binding and loosing that give spiritual jurisdiction to the community.

In the Book of Acts the dramatic discipline of Ananias and Sapphira (Acts 5:1-11) is a warning to the entire church, and the accounts of Simon Magus and Elymas the magician portray aspects of discipline (Acts 8:24; 13:8-11).

PAULINE LETTERS. In the Pauline letters we see the most frequent guidance regarding questions of discipline. The passages warrant careful exegetical examination, but that is beyond our purposes here. We shall simply note the scope of these materials.

Romans 16:17 says, "Mark them who cause divisions and offenses contrary to the doctrine which we have learned; and avoid them."

In 1 Corinthians 5:1-13, there is an incest case in the church with instructions "to deliver such an one unto Satan for the destruction of the flesh" (v. 5) since "a little leaven leaveneth the whole lump" (v. 6), which must therefore be "purged" (v. 7), and thus we are not to "company with" (v. 9) such persons as fornicators, drunkards, railers, or the covetous, not even to eat with them (v. 11). "Therefore, put away from among yourselves that wicked person" (v. 13).

In 2 Corinthians 2:5-11 we find instructions to forgive and love those who cause grief but repent, and not to compound the punishment "lest perhaps such a one be swallowed up with overmuch sorrow" (v. 7).

"Warn them that are unruly" is found in 1 Thessalonians 5:14.

To discipline the idle, 2 Thessalonians 3:6-15 says, "Withdraw yourselves from every brother that walketh disorderly, and not after the tradition that he received of us" (v. 6). "If any man obey not our word . . . have no company with him, that he may be ashamed. Yet count him not as an enemy, but admonish him as a brother" (vv. 14, 15).

Additional passages on the subject are found in Galatians 2:11-21; Ephesians 5:11; 1 Timothy 1:20; 5:19, 20; 6:4, 5; 2 Timothy 3:2-5; Titus 2:15; 3:10, 11; and 2 Corinthians 6:14-16.

NON-PAULINE LETTERS. Other New Testament materials likewise reflect practices of ecclesiastical discipline. The issue appears in Hebrews in connection with those who may be losing faith (3:12-16; 6:4-8; 10:26-30; 12:5-17), in some epistles where issues of false teachers are arising (2 Pet. 2:1, 2, 9-19; 1 John 4:1-3; 2 John 7:11; Jude 4, 8-23), and in one instance in a warning about the abuse of discipline (3 John 9, 10).

These passages may not provide formulas or any specific structure of church order,[9] but their thrust seems clear. Their weight moved Charles Deweese to write to his Baptist brethren:

We cannot justify our prevalent tendency to by-pass these passages relating to discipline. . . . To pretend that serious offenses do not exist is a slap in the face of disciplinary patterns advocated by Jesus and New Testament leaders and writers.[10]

THE POST-APOSTOLIC CHURCH. Discipline, and controversy about it, was prominent in the life of the post-apostolic church. It was a crisis time for the community, cut loose from the roots of apostolic presence, encountering a hostile world, and commissioned with a global agenda. The concern of the church was not merely to keep recalcitrant members in line or to separate the sheep from the goats. At stake was the "very life-style of the church."[11]

Cecil Cadoux has noted four major problems faced by the early church that contributed to the tensions and developments in regard to ecclesiastical discipline: idolatry, heresy, immorality, and worldliness.[12] Idolatry was persistent in the syncretistic world of Rome, and it became a critical issue as the church struggled with what to do about those who "lapsed" and compromised their faith by participation in pagan ceremonies.

The condemnation of heresy was vital for the young church seeking to adhere to the "apostles' doctrine." The Christological controversies, for example, were central to the character of the new faith, with little room

DISCIPLINE IN CHURCH HISTORY

for compromise or accommodation. Such struggles were not new to the church. The Book of Acts recounts the battles over the character of the gospel, and later epistles are replete with warnings about false teachers. The theological debates of these initial centuries were often critical and certainly always fierce. Ignatius, an early church father, suggested that Docetists (who opposed the idea that Christ had a body and suffered physically) should be neither spoken to nor listened to but shunned like wild beasts. John the apostle reportedly fled once from the public bath when he discovered that the heretic Cerinthus was there.

Ethical standards of the new faith were equally under siege, and the church felt compelled to take a firm stand on issues ranging from sexual excesses to infanticide. The commitment to a new creation meant that much of the culture and entertainment of the Roman world was not compatible with a heavenly citizenship.[13] Participation in public games and theater attendance were just two activities prohibited for members of the community of faith.

This was the context in which the doctrines and practices of church discipline were hammered out.

Preventive discipline: selective admission. In the early years of the church, when neither the Christian faith nor the faithful were popular and when persecution was a prominent feature of the life of the believers, little attention was given to standards for admission to the community. There was no need for concern about insincere members. Entry was by simple declaration of faith and baptism. As persecution waned and larger proportions of the population were attracted to the church, the question emerged regarding the qualifications for membership. Soon one of the major forms of preventive discipline developed: standards and procedures for membership examination and instruction. Not only were there theological expectations and demands for personal faith, but certain kinds of conduct and even occupations were bars to membership:

Panderers, prostitutes, idol-makers, idol-priests, actors, charioteers, gladiators, sorcerers, and in some places and to some extent, soldiers and magistrates were not admitted.[14]

Gradually specific forms of preparation were developed for catechumens, the candidates for baptism. In the Clementine *Recognitions,* for example, we discover that the people of Caesarea were invited to undergo a three-month course under Zacheus, the bishop. Other places involved instruction of often a year or two.[15]

Such caution regarding admittance reflects the same concerns involved in questions of church discipline: the church's purity, the guarding of its witness, and the character of its membership.

Corrective discipline. Instruction alone proved insufficient, however, and the church soon faced the question of its responsibility in regard to members. Sin was as much a reality in the early church as in apostolic or modern times.

There was actually no dispute about the duty or practice of the church to exercise the power of expulsion.[16] That was a presumption and a practice of the church. Discipline was applied regularly by the early church to those who by thought or conduct had, in effect, already removed themselves from the community. Open sin was simply inconsistent with the new creation.

The critical issue in the first centuries of

the Christian church was not expulsion, but whether or not one who had been expelled for heresy, idolatry, or immorality could, upon repentance, be readmitted to the community. There were some rigorists who contended that there could be no post-baptismal forgiveness, no readmittance. Others differed and the debates raged throughout the second century. Reconciliation was severely restricted during the first two centuries. But late in the second century, as expressed in works such as the *Shepherd of Hermas*, it was generally agreed that there could be one further opportunity for a reinstatement for the lapsed based on a public confession of sin before the congregation. As Tertullian wrote in *De Paenitentia*, God leaves the door of forgiveness "slightly ajar." This second chance was the last; *exomologesis* could not be repeated.[17] But there was great concern with the threat of laxity in the church. Many such as Tertullian fought hard against any lessening of this one-forgiveness limit.

In the Eastern church by the second century there was a clear stipulation that there could be only one post-baptismal reconciliation, and even this opportunity was excluded in the cases of apostasy, adultery, and homicide.[18] Any restoration was based on a *public* confession and repentance. John McNeill notes, "In the early church, the chief feature of discipline was its public character." The congregation was involved, and the penitent made his confession before all.

By the third century, a fairly rigorous series of acts of penance were required for restoration, including fasting, wearing of sackcloth and ashes, weeping, groaning, and throwing oneself at the feet of the presbyters pleading for restoration. Kenneth Scott Latourette describes the scene of a penance:

A place was appointed in which penitents stood and mourned until the completion of the service. They then cast themselves prostrate on the ground with groans and lamentations. The bishop, weeping, also cast himself on the ground, and the congregation wept and groaned. The bishop then rose, offered a prayer for the penitents, and dismissed them.[19]

THE MEDIEVAL MODEL. Between the second and sixth centuries the system became increasingly formalized, with rites and activities of penance systematized by synodical decrees with ever-increasing formalities and gradations. Eventually there was an enrollment in an order of penitents (ordo paenitentium) either voluntarily or by ecclesiastical decree, with specific regimens and penalties for offenses. The one-time restriction on restoration continued unabated.

In the Eastern church there were special classes of penitents: "mourners" were excluded from the church building but gathered in the forecourt or narthex to plead with the faithful; "hearers" were allowed to listen to the Scriptures but then were dismissed before communion; the "kneelers" were also dismissed before communion but with a blessing and laying on of hands by the bishop; the "bystanders" were allowed to stay through the service but not partake of communion.

During these early centuries the tendency was to "get tough," but the process of church discipline was undergoing significant changes.

Until the sixth century, the lay congregation was involved in reconciliation of the lapsed, but there was a gradual shift from the laity to the bishop, and eventually to the priest. By the end of the sixth century, the new customs of confessing to a priest had led to penitential codes to guide priests in imposing penance. For example, according to one code ascribed to Egbert of York, spreading slander deserved seven years of penance and swearing by a consecrated cross merited three years. Discipline became highly impersonal, institutional, formal, and mechanical.

The shift was not only from the laity to the priesthood but from public confession to private confession. In the third century, church fathers noted that the high visibility of confession and the rigors of penance tended to discourage open confession and perhaps even encouraged people to delay baptism so they would not be caught with more than one post-baptismal sin. But the major occasion for the shift was the influence of the confessional practices of the Celts in Ireland who had never evolved a public penitential system but had relied on private confession to the priest. The Celtic ideas came into Europe in the sixth century and began to carry the day in spite of synodical pressures to resist the changes. By the twelfth century, the practice of private confession became the norm and was finally required of all believers at least once a year. The Lateran Council in 1215 encoded these changes:

Every *fidelis* of either sex shall after the attainment of years of discretion confess his sins with all fidelity to his own priest at least once in the year.

While public penance did not die out, it became known as "solemn penance" and was imposed only for notorious and scandalous crimes.[20]

The rule of only one reconciliation was also now effectively gone. As confession became an increasingly private matter between the penitent and a priest, the whole milieu for enforcing such a rule was no longer available.

It is also clear that the initial concerns for a pure church and for restoration to those who truly repented had largely given way to an emphasis not on contrition but on acts of penitence. This formalized system in turn gave way to the private confessional system common in the Roman Catholic church today.

The attempts to maintain a pure, disciplined church not only failed, but the very system of penitence that evolved became a cause of the Reformation. The missing element was the gospel's message of the good news of grace and release. Discipline was no longer about discipleship.

THE REFORMATION. One observer noted that there was a "strong accent on church discipline in the Reformation."[21] Discipline, preaching, and the sacraments became known as signs of the true church with discipline as the "third mark of the church."[22]

The Reformers retained the Roman practice of private confession under the administration of the priest, but they had harsh words for many aspects of auricular confession and the abuses of penance. They put more emphasis on absolution and less on contrition or any works of penance lest there be a confusion between grace and works.[23] Calvin did confirm a role for "private confession to his own pastor" whenever a person is so troubled "by a sense of his sins that he cannot obtain relief without the help of others." He warned, however, that people should be free to confess only as they felt it necessary and should not be forced or tricked into enumerating all their sins.[24]

LUTHERANISM. The Lutheran wing of the Reformation showed little interest in formal structures of church discipline. Though Luther wrote a treatise on the subject of the ban and occasionally utilized church discipline, he rejected the ban itself, expressed reservations about any involvement of the secular authorities in enforcing church discipline, and never formally instituted procedures for church discipline. The first manuals for church order written at Wittenburg in 1533 contained no provisions for penance, confession, or the ban. Luther remarked on one occasion that he "would gladly institute" church discipline, but "it's not the time for it." He once yearned: "If only there were people who would allow themselves to be disciplined." One form of discipline Luther did practice and advocate was exclusion from the Lord's Supper: "Discipline is above all a discipline from the Lord's Supper."

After Luther's death, church discipline in the Lutheran territories emerged and involved secular authorities through the consistory, a government-related organization. The practice permitted the minister to exclude penitents from communion, but excommunication, fines, or punishments were only meted out by the consistory.

ZWINGLI. In the Swiss and southern German regions, discipline was much more prominent. Zwingli devoted an article to the ban in his *Auslegung und Begrundung der Schlussreden*. Here, there was a deliberate involvement of civil authorities. In Zwingli's system, the civil magistrate functioned much like church elders in the implementation of discipline, and the power of excommunication was in the hands of the magistrate. In 1525 a tribunal consisting of both church and civic authorities was empowered to investigate disciplinary situations, and its recommendations went to the secular authorities. Civil penalties were a prominent part of the system of discipline.

THE CALVINISTS. Within the mainstream of the Reformation, Calvin probably went the furthest in implementing church discipline. In the *Fourth Book of the Institutes,* Calvin declared:

As the saving doctrine of Christ is the soul of the church, so discipline forms the ligaments that connect the members together, and keep each in its proper place. Whoever, therefore, either desires the abolition of discipline, or obstructs its restoration, . . . they certainly promote the entire dissolution of the church.[25]

Discipline was no luxury. "If no society, indeed no house which has even a small family, can be kept in proper condition without discipline, it is much more necessary in the church." Calvin even made the implementation of church discipline a condition of his return to Geneva in 1541.

Calvin drew specifically on Matthew 18, noting that discipline was dependent on "the power of the keys and upon spiritual jurisdiction." He taught that discipline's "first foundation" is "private admonition," but pastors and presbyters are to "be especially watchful to do this" for their duty is not only to preach, but to "warn and exhort in every house." When anyone "stubbornly rejects such admonitions" after a second admonishment "in the presence of witnesses," then "Christ commands that he be called to the tribunal of the church . . . and there be admonished as by public authority." If he is not thus subdued but perseveres in his evil, then "Christ commands that, as a despiser of the church, he be removed from the believers' fellowship."

The Reformation, particularly in its Calvinist expressions, left a legacy of discipline to the Scottish Presbyterians and the Puritans[26] where "the discipline of Geneva found its most congenial soil."

THE ANABAPTISTS. "The Anabaptists were the fullest exemplar of a pervasive sixteenth century phenomenon: attempts to purify the church through renewed church discipline."[27] In the left wing of the Reformation the concerns for a pure, voluntary, and holy church were central, and discipline was most clearly practiced. Though Anabaptists varied considerably in their implementation, church discipline was a mark of all their communities. Rooted in Scripture, they took their practices directly from the words of Jesus in Matthew 18:15-17 that they called the "Rule of Christ."

Menno Simmons wrote three tracts on the subject, and the second of seven articles in the Scheitheim Confession of 1527 was on the ban:

We are agreed as follows on the ban: The ban shall be employed with all those who have given themselves to the Lord, to walk in His commandments . . . and who are called brethren or sisters, and yet who slip sometime and fall into error and sin. . . . The same shall be admonished twice in secret and the third time openly disciplined or banned according to the command of Christ.

Behind the practice of discipline were three basic convictions about the church. First, the church was a voluntary community with adult baptism as a sign of a personal, voluntary witness to faith. Second was the understanding of the corporate character of the community. The church was a fellowship, a brotherhood of persons bound to one another. Third was the conviction of the call to purity of life for a redeemed, regenerate people.

Therefore, baptism was a "covenantal ordinance of moral intention in the context of the believing brotherhood, both a pledge to God and to one's fellow believers to live piously and in brotherly fellowship." Holiness and corporateness were to be marks of the believer. The world might contain a mixture of wheat and tares but not the church. The goal was the restoration of churches as holy Christian communities.

The two Anabaptist contributions to the Reformation milieu, adult baptism and the Rule of Christ, were direct products of this commitment. Conrad Grebel, an early Anabaptist leader, said that the goal was to "create a Christian church with the help of Christ and His Rule as we find it instituted in Matthew 18 and practiced in the Epistles."[28] These two were inseparable. Grebel insisted, "We understand that even an adult is not to be baptised apart from Christ's rule of binding and loosing."[29] Likewise, Balthasar Hubmaier claimed that adult baptism would be "no better than infant baptism had been if fraternal admonition and excommunication did not go along with it."[30]

This discipline was exclusively a church practice, effective only within the local, visible congregations or brotherhoods and related solely to religious, moral, and church affairs. There was to be no involvement of civil authorities and no civil punishment. The civil society according to Hubmaier was properly one of wheat and tares, and heretics should be left alone by civil authority. Hubmaier insisted that the proper use of the ban had been lost in Christian history because it had been applied to civil affairs.[31]

If for the Roman church the test was "No bishop, no church," it is clear that for Anabaptists, it was "No discipline, no church."[32]

POST-REFORMATION CHURCHES. The ideas of Calvin, Hubmaier, Simmons, and Luther played themselves out in many of the newer religious groups both on the continent and in America. These concepts are reflected in the Methodists, Quakers, and English Baptists. Since many of these groups, like the Anabaptists, sought to create a biblical community of regenerate members, their disciplinary practices often have more in common with the Anabaptists than with Luther or even Calvin.

The Methodists had a vigorous church discipline in the early days. Wesley organized his followers into "societies" and classes with leaders:

I called together all leaders of the classes . . . and desired that each would make a particular inquiry into the behavior of those he saw weekly; they did so: many disorderly walkers were detected; some turned away from the evil of their ways: some were put away from us: many saw it with fear, and rejoiced unto God with reverence. . . .

It is the business of a class leader:
  To see each person in his class, once a week at the least, in order

    To enquire how their soul prospers
    To advise, reprove, comfort, or exhort, as occasion may require
    To receive what they are willing to give towards the relief of the poor. . . .

In American Methodism, the class leaders were described by one contemporary source as "watchers on the walls of our spiritual Zion," and Matthew 18 was regularly applied. The class leaders were supervised by a circuit rider who checked on them and tried any who would not be reconciled by Matthew 18.

The discipline was intended to provide self-protection without which "the church would be like a field without fences, exposed to invasion from every quarter."

Examples are numerous: Isaac Conger, a Tennessee circuit rider, reported that on one trip he "turned out two for not being in fellowship with each other and telling storyes" and that evening he "regulated" a man for "whipping his wife." Methodists were brought before the church for a variety of offenses including immorality, drunkenness, dishonest land deals, selling unsound merchandise, lying, and breach of marriage contract. But far from resisting such practices, they were seen as quite appropriate. One bishop tells the story of a man who insisted he be tried for an offense and protested a lenient sentence.[33]

The English Baptists reflected many of the Anabaptist views of the church and discipline. Like Anabaptists they saw the church as a voluntary, visible, and holy community. The London Confession of 1644 spoke of the church as a "spirituall Kingdom," a "company of visible saints, called and separated from the world" by profession of faith and baptism and "joynd to the Lord, and each other, by mutual agreement. . . ."[34]

This community viewed discipline as central to its life. One creed noted that two marks of the true church were discipline and government administered by pastors whom the congregation elected. John Smyth, an early Baptist leader, spoke of the duties of church leaders:

The cheef care of every member must be to watch over his brother . . . in bearing one another's burden . . . admonishing the unruly, comforting the

feeble mynded . . . admonishing the excommunicate . . . restoring them that are fallen.[35]

The Somerset Confession, Article XXV,
lists commandments critical to the lives of
believers. Number 9 notes a duty of reproof;
Number 17, "publick rebuke to publick of-
fenders"; and No. 16 declares: "Private admonition to a brother offending another, and
if not prevailing, to take one or two more, if
he hear not them, then tell it to the church;
and if he hear not them to be accounted as a
heathen and a publican."
This reliance on Matthew 18 was common.
John Smyth said such practices were necessary not because the church arrogantly assumed perfection, but precisely because the
church knew that each person was subject
to sin; thus the process of correction was
necessary. Matthew 18 was strictly followed,
and one might be subject to rebuke if one
brought up an issue before the church that
had not been first discussed privately. Regular meetings were set aside for "discipline"
with the frequency varying from monthly to
annually. For example, the Particular Baptist
meetings at Broadmead were held monthly
and limited to church members, who were
expected to attend. The church at Canter-
bury declared "that in case any member neglect meetings as are appointed for
discipline, they shall send cause by some
member that day or otherwise declare it
themselves the next first day, and upon failure of this, the person shall be reprovable."
The issues that came before the church to
apply Matthew 18 included unmanageable
debt, slander, theft, adultery, neglect of family affairs, failure to attend worship, refusing
to contribute offerings, causing dissension,
and heresy.[36] But ultimately only one cause,
a failure to hear the church, resulted in ex-

clusion. It was not the sin, but the refusal to repent and be reconciled that occasioned the church's severe action. The disciplining charge usually included the clause that the person had "despised the counsel of the church."

Where excommunication did occur, the names were distributed to all the churches, but the excommunication did not involve worldly business or civil society. In fact, continued contact for encouragement and reconciliation was expected.

Baptists in America practiced discipline nearly identical with their English counterparts. Baptists guarded carefully the membership of the church, demanding evidence of conversion and refusing admittance to anyone transferring who did not bring a letter indicating they were in good standing. Churches were known to complain directly if another church accepted one who had not given satisfaction to a prior church. Membership was further guarded by the covenant to which members assented.

Discipline played a strong role in enforcing the covenant and the moral life of the communities. Matthew 18 was strictly applied and churches would often not consider a matter until the first two steps had been undertaken. Far from being legalistic and quick to judge, some studies have shown churches exercised great patience and mercy. In a case study of one church, only after applying Matthew 18 to no avail would the church appoint a committee to seek "to labor with and try to win him." Only then would the congregation vote on excommunication. In a study of five frontier Baptist churches from 1781 to 1860, 1,636 individual cases were heard, many of them more than once and often five or six times, covering a wide variety of conduct such as drinking too much, not paying debts, "promising and not performing," free-masonry, defaming a neighbor, and false teaching.

The practices in America and other portions of the New World developed in a different context from that of either medieval Europe or the Reformation. The growing acceptance of the separation of church and state dramatically shifted discipline for those traditions that historically had sought state assistance. Discipline became a matter that clearly carried exclusive spiritual jurisdiction. In most of the world pluralism and secularism resulted in problems for church discipline not faced by previous cultures.

CONCLUSIONS

This brief overview of the history of church discipline and its biblical roots leads to a number of important conclusions:

1. There is a clear biblical warrant both in specific texts and in general teachings to call for churches to develop an understanding and practice of appropriate church discipline.

2. The practices of church discipline in church history have frequently been mandated and shaped by specific contexts of the church's life at any given time.

3. Fundamental theological convictions about the nature and governance of the church and forgiveness, to name only two, underlie specific practices and concepts of church discipline.

4. Reform movements that seek to recover the simplicity of the church and its biblical basis tend to develop church forms that give a more prominent place to church discipline.

Whatever the motives and styles chosen, there seems to be an inherent possibility of abuse. The practice and structure of church discipline have often resulted in actions that are inconsistent with great biblical themes.

[1]Herbert J. A. Bouman, "Biblical Presuppositions for Church Discipline," *Concordia Theological Monthly,* July 1959, 503-515.

NOTES

[2]Gen. 12:1, 2; 17:1, 2; Exod. 19:3-6; 20:1-21; Isa. 1:1-20; 58:13, 14. See Maynard Shelley, ed., *Studies in Church Discipline* (Newton, Kans.: Faith & Life, 1958), 80ff.

[3]Some scholars have noted parallels between early church excommunication and the *cherem* or curse placed upon evil for its destruction (Josh. 6:16-21; 1 Sam. 15:1-4, 32, 33) and parallels between the later practices of the ban in the diaspora with the interdiction and excommunication of Christian history.

[4]See Marlin Jeschke, "Toward an Evangelical Conception of Corrective Church Discipline" (Ph.D. diss., Northwestern University, 1965). Three levels of Talmudic discipline were (1) the *nezifah,* a rebuke or censure that imposed a one-day discipline (or seven days in the Palestinian Talmud) during which the party was to go home and carry on no business or entertainment; (2) the *niddui,* a short-term excommunication applied for twenty-four different offenses, mostly violations of Mosaic law or insubordination of rabbinical authority, that required the party to wear mourning habit and refrain from bathing or cutting his hair. It prohibited any one from eating with him, and only his wife and children could have contact with him during the seven-day period (or thirty days in the Palestinian Talmud). (3) The most severe was the *cherem,* the curse that was imposed on one who refused to amend his ways after three *nidduis.* The *cherem* was imposed by a community of at least ten persons. The *cherem* was a ban in which the person was considered dead, cut off from the community. Often the rituals even involved a symbolic bier and the extinguishing of lights. The *cherem* was revocable, however.

[5]Ibid.

[6]Critics of church discipline frequently note the account in John 8 of Jesus' encounter with the woman taken in adultery and other teachings and stories that model an understanding of forgiveness that cuts through the rigidity of Talmudic "penance."

[7]Harold O. J. Brown, "The Role of Discipline in the Church," *The Covenant Quarterly,* Aug. 1983, 51.

[8]Bouman, 511, 513.

[9]Eduard Schweizer, *Church Order in the New Testament* (London: SCM Press, 1961), suggests that while there is no one church order in the New Testament (p. 13), the "New Testament is unanimous that the church never lives without order" (p. 194).

[10]Charles Deweese, *A Community of Believers* (Valley Forge, Pa.: Judson Press, 1978), 69.

[11]Frank Senn, "Structures of Penance and the Ministry of Reconciliation," *Lutheran Quarterly,* Aug. 1973, 270.

[12]Cecil Cadoux, *The Early Church and the World* (Edinburgh: T. & T. Clark, 1925).

[13]Origen had suggested that Christians should "sever and break themselves away from those who are aliens to the commonwealth of God and strangers to his covenants, in order that they may carry out their heavenly citizenship."

[14]Cadoux, 601.

[15]Ibid., 475.

[16]The *Shepherd of Hermas* spoke of a need for the church to be purged of unworthy members so it could become "one body, one thought, one mind, one faith, one love."

[17]These ideas lasted for some centuries, although the Third Council of Toledo (A.D. 589) was the last to insist on only one post baptismal reconciliation.

[18]Some went even further in barring forgiveness. For example, the Spanish Council of Elvira in A.D. 306 listed nineteen sins for which reconciliation could never be granted. Montanism was a protest against laxity that had crept into the church. "The Church can forgive sins, but I will not do so, lest others also commit sin," declared one writer (from *Oracle of the Paraclete,* preserved by Tertullian, *De pud.* 21.7). The Montanists fought views such as that of Dionysius, bishop of Corinth (ca. A.D. 170) who had declared, "All those who are converted from any fall, be it error or even heresy, should be received." See Bernherd Poschmann, *Penance and the Anointing of the Sick,* trans. F. Courtney (New York: Herder & Herder, 1964). St. Cyprian, in his treatise on *The Lapsed,* trans. Maurice Bevenot, S.J. (Westminster, Md.: The Newman Press, 1957), complains of a too-easy restoration of members after idolatry as a "new source of disaster" created by an evil masquerading as compassion, with the result that "a deceptive readmission to communion is being granted, a reconciliation which is null and void. . . . What remorse they had has

been snatched from their breasts, the gravity and enormity of their crime has been blotted from their memory. . . . People coming back from the altars of Satan approach Our Lord's sacred body, their hands still foul and reeking. . . ."

[19]Kenneth Scott Latourette, *A History of Christianity* (New York: Harper & Row, 1953), 217.

[20]Henry Charles Lea, *A History of Auricular Confession and Indulgences in the Latin Church,* vol. 1 (Philadelphia: Lea Bros., 1896), 36, 37.

[21]F. Burton Nelson, "Comment," *The Covenant Quarterly,* Aug. 1977, 1.

[22]Eugene P. Heideman, "Disciples and Identity," *Reformed Review,* Fall 1981, 18.

[23]As to contrition, for example, Luther warned that he had no objection to an examination to see if one was truly contrite, "Just so no one becomes so bold . . . that he claims to have sufficient contrition," and he warned that the best "satisfaction" for sin was to sin no more. "This kind of satisfaction is rarely mentioned: we think to pay for everything through assigned prayers." E. T. Bachman, ed., "The Sacrament of Penance," *Luther's Works, Word and Sacrament I,* vol. 35 (Philadelphia: Muhlenburg Press, 1960), 11, 21.

[24]John Calvin, "Private Confession in the Cure of Souls," in *Institutes of the Christian Religion,* vol. 1 (Grand Rapids: Eerdman's, 1975), 544, 545.

[25]Cited by Marlin Jeschke, *Discipling the Brother* (Scottdale, Pa.: Herald Press, 1972), 32.

[26]The Puritan Confession of 1589 set forth its discipline that tracked Matthew 18 and emphasized the role of the congregation.

[27]Jean Runzo, "Communal Discipline in the Early Anabaptist Communities . . ." (Ph.D. diss., University of Michigan, 1978).

[28]*Conrad Grebel's Programmatic Letters* (Scottdale, Pa.: Herald Press, 1970), 27.

[29]Ibid., 29.

[30]Balthasar Hubmaier, *Schriften,* eds. Von Gunnar Westin and Torsten Bergsten (Gütersloher: G. Mohn, 1962), 338.

[31]Anabaptist ideas had some significant influence even on the mainstream of the Reformation. The Anabaptists and Reformation leaders, such as Zwingli, Bucer, and

Calvin carried on heated debates, and Bucer seems to have been influenced by his exchanges with Anabaptists and to have influenced his former assistant, John Calvin. Calvin later wrote in regard to his own practices: "We do not deny the ban is not only useful but essential to the church. Yea, what these unfortunate and thankless popely [the Anabaptists] teach about it, they learned from us, only their ignorance and presumption have ruined the doctrine which we keep pure." See Kenneth R. Davis, "No Discipline, No Church: An Anabaptist Contribution to the Reformed Tradition," *Sixteenth Century Journal* 13 (1982), 4.

[32]Davis, "No Discipline, No Church," 58.

[33]See Liston O. Mills, "The Relationship of Discipline to Pastoral Care in Frontier Churches, 1800-1850," *Pastoral Psychology,* Dec. 1965, for a discussion of this area.

[34]William Lumpkin, *Baptist Confessions of Faith* (Philadelphia: Judson Press, 1959), 165

[35]"Principles and Inferences," in *The Works of John Smyth* (Cambridge: Cambridge University Press, 1915), 261.

[36]For an excellent discussion see James R. Lynch, "English Baptist Discipline to 1740," *Foundations,* Apr.-June 1975, 121-135.

4

DISCIPLINE: A RELIC OR A REQUIREMENT?

Discipline is a privilege of church membership.
Laury Eck[1]

If the machinery of church discipline is revved up and allowed to roll over the weak, the untidy, and the indifferent in the church, irreparable damage can be done.[2]

"Church discipline is to be considered the normal church life," concluded Marlin Jeschke in his study of the history of church discipline.[3] That may be, but if so, the modern church must be severely abnormal. Consider the observation of Emil Brunner:

The function of church discipline has . . . to a very great extent fallen into disuse. . . . The Church ought to know, however, that the absence of any kind of church discipline inevitably gives the impression that to belong or not to belong to the Church comes to the same thing in the end, and makes no difference in practical life. . . .[4]

Most of us are familiar with the stories of the authority of the church and its power of discipline in a former age. In medieval times, church authority was so strong that Pope Gregory VII (1073-1085) could by the power of ecclesiastical discipline force Henry IV to stand as a penitent in the snows outside the castle at Canossa begging the pope to cancel his excommunication.[5]

But church discipline is by no means a mere medieval relic of an authoritarian church. As we have seen, it was a prominent feature of almost every age of the church and of our own American tradition, so much so that church historian George Marsden could insist that "church discipline . . . is as American as apple pie."[6] Yet such discipline is rarely seen in today's church.

Few are eager to return to the days of Hildebrand, with preachers or elders meddling and bossing others around, or to have penitents mourning in the entryways of our churches, begging us to intercede for them. In fact, the very words *church discipline* rarely invite positive images to mind. The general attitude is "good riddance"; it is something whose time has passed, like witch-hunts and stocks in the main squares of Massachusetts towns. The idea of "shunning," practiced in Anabaptist circles, seems as antique as an Amish buggy.

Understood biblically, however, church discipline is not the narrow exercise of a private morality, not a way of ridding the church of "sinners" so that only the pure are left in a church without spot or wrinkle, nor a means of dealing with "embarrassments" in the church. It is not chiefly about excommunication. Rather, church discipline includes all the ways and means by which the church invites and exhorts persons to live in faithfulness and obedience to Christ. The word *discipline* comes from the Latin *discipulus,* "pupil," and refers to that which corrects, molds, or perfects.[7] Therefore, it embraces many dimensions, including the preaching of the Word. Centuries ago, Clement declared: "A horse is guided by a bit, and a bull is guided by a yoke . . . but man is transformed by the Word."[8] Discipline also includes teaching ministries, exhortation, counseling, encouraging, enabling. Discipline is part of discipling. To separate discipling from discipline is not only to tear words from their etymological common roots, but from their organic relationship.

The fact that we think of church discipline exclusively in terms of "kicking people out," is a sign of the paucity of broader discipling in our churches today.

The phrase "church discipline" may legitimately refer to those acts of the church that specifically hold persons accountable and that are exercises of the spiritual authority of the church.[9] We use the word *discipline* in our families in much the same way. But it would be dangerous to wrench discipline in the church from its roots of discipleship and discipling. Discipleship is at the core of Christian faith, demand and discipline inherent within it.[10]

Discipline for discipleship will be predominantly preventive, educative, enabling. But there are times when it will be corrective. It will include judgment. A community that takes its character seriously and disciplines will insist on repentance, it will refuse to let people dodge their callings, and in some instances it may ultimately require dismissal from the community of faith.

WHY HAS CORRECTIVE CHURCH DISCIPLINE DECLINED?

If church discipline has been widely practiced in church history, why has it become so quaint and peculiar? Why was the decision of the Collinsville church so newsworthy? Why have we abandoned discipline?

The reasons are doubtless many, but we can note a few factors that have contributed to modern skepticism, even in the church, about corrective church discipline.

ABUSES! Much of the reluctance to return "to the days of yore" is because of concerns about the practice of church discipline by previous generations. We have already noted some practices of the church that seem to most of us both tragic and unbiblical. The complaints, though often drawing on distortions or exceptions in those earlier practices, do raise legitimate concerns. What are the alleged abuses of church discipline? Here are a baker's dozen:[11]

1. It was often *too legalistic.* Church discipline became the strict imposition of a set of rules that were perceived as defining the nature of faith and Christian life, almost exclusively negative in form, and tending to create the impression that faith was chiefly conformity and avoidance of sin.[12]

2. It *lacked a redemptive focus.* Church discipline was more interested in getting rid of persons than reclaiming them. The sentencing, the judgment, became the end rather than a means. When such discipline lacks a redemptive focus it simply mirrors the world where the "natural reaction is to shun, to condemn, to punish, to drive away. . . ."[13]

3. It often became *highly impersonal,* especially where it was administered by formal ecclesiastical courts, thus lacking the love and care of the community so essential to restoration and forgiveness.

4. It *trivialized discipleship* by focusing on minor externals. It forgot beams and saw only the motes; its norms were often products of a particular subculture, rather than touching the central attributes of Christian

life. It confused mores with holiness.

5. It sometimes became a *tool for expressing personal animosities.* An example is the refusal of John Wesley (in his early days in America) to serve communion to a young woman who did not return his affections.

6. It became a means for pastors to *get rid of troublemakers.* Recently in Ohio, a Baptist church pastor called a summary meeting to expel a member who had criticized the pastor's decisions, charging that she was guilty of being contentious and divisive. It is like the pastor who, when asked if there had been any additions to his church since the last annual meeting, replied, "No, but there have been some blessed subtractions."

7. It was used to *enforce a narrow behavioral conformity.* Discipline became a tool for keeping everyone in line, a socio-political weapon. It often put a premium on obedience, encouraging a dependency syndrome that suffocated and stifled individual growth and prophetic witness. Since authorities, whether individuals or majorities, have such an uncertain track record on truth, we ought to be cautious in penalizing nonconformity, which just as often as not may be a mark of the unique people of God.

8. It was a way to *get rid of embarrassing problems or people.* Rather than risk ministry to them, "church discipline" became a shortcut to rid the church of the embarrassment quickly, cleansing the body of a moral flaw and thus avoiding any taint. It was really the opposite of a commitment to persons.

9. It was essentially *negative.* It became a sort of "search and destroy" mission, ever eager to identify sin, but less concerned with spiritual growth, grace, and affirmation.

10. It was often *theologically and biblically suspect.* In both substance and administra-

tion, it often failed to give sufficient attention to doctrines of forgiveness, to the sufficiency of grace, to the acknowledgment of the universality of sin; and it reflected a misperception of the role of the church.[14]

11. It was often *dangerously authoritarian.* It easily became a justification for ministers and church leaders to rule with authoritarian styles. Persons unable to cope with challenges, who are weak leaders, take refuge in "church disciplinary" authority and cling to this as a rationale for their domineering styles.

12. It was too exclusively *hierarchical.* It often functioned to detract from broader concepts of mutual accountability instead of submitting "one to another" under mutual discipline.

13. It forced impossible and dangerous *hairsplitting.* It became entangled with the inherent problems and dangers of line-drawing. What "sins" call for discipline? What conduct requires *public* discipline? Since we are all sinners, how can we single out some of us? Are we not in danger of weighing sins, having lists of "serious" sins and not-so-serious ones—a hierarchy of sins? Won't we inevitably begin focusing on "public" and "notorious" sins, while ignoring the equally destructive but less measurable and identifiable ones?

Were there abuses and problems such as these? Of course there were, and critics both within and without the church love to cite the worst cases. But we might ponder the observation of Geddes MacGregor in *The Coming Reformation:*

To abandon discipline because it has sometimes been ill-administered is as unwarranted as it would be to abandon worship on the ground that it has sometimes been ill-conducted. *The relax-*

ation of discipline has often more absurd results than ever attended its excesses.[15]

There are doubtless theological problems not only with many of the historic practices but with the way church discipline is administered in some churches today. Few would deny that church discipline is a dangerous task. Judging is risky business both before man and God. There are dangers in the role of "judgment" implicit in corrective church discipline, the kind that Kenneth Kirk called "penal discipline," which cuts off the weak, as opposed to "pastoral discipline," which "strengthens and encourages" the weak.[16] Gregory the Great had similarly warned of excessive judgment that causes sinners to become dejected and fall into despair.[17]

Some of our anxiety about discipline today is rooted in our contemporary confusion about the church, about authority, and even about God. Our age is disconcerted about issues of authority generally, and the same is true within the church. This confusion surfaces at multiple levels, whether it be questions about subjection to any authority, the authority of Scripture, tensions between personalism and life in community, or the potential for discovering any truth upon which one may rest and base an authority. If the church knows no authority and believes it possesses none, even as to its own commitment to faith and life, then church discipline is preempted. The issue of authority is also related to the issues of judgment, when and how judging is appropriate, and in what cases it falls within the biblical warning against judging: "Judge not that ye be not judged" (Matt. 7:1).

This confusion about authority bears directly on the issues of leadership and fellowship in our day. In *Clergy in the Crossfire,*

Donald Smith sketches out the dilemmas of the modern clergy caught in the "crossfire" of contemporary social and religious changes that have resulted in confusion about pastoral identity, role, and authority.[18] Smith suggests that the result is a clergy unclear of its place not only in the world, but in the church. Our understanding of the nature of pastoral leadership today is fuzzy, with implications across the whole spectrum of church life. "Greg" notes in his book that "any leader who plans to lead must give commands."[19]

This confusion within the church's pastoral leadership spills across the whole leadership of the church and has direct implications for its capacity to teach or practice any form of church discipline.

The confusion about authority probably has something to do with the prevalent lack of convictions about values and principles. Where there are no convictions, no deeply held norms, no assurance, there will always be a laissez-faire environment. When people feel they must hide or apologize for their convictions, then church discipline will be untenable.

It is also clear some of the resistance to explore appropriate church discipline is rooted in our own anxieties, fears, and sin. Some are ignorant of biblical teachings on the subject; some wear blinders to the moral and theological issues in the life of the church today; many are confused with a false image of kindness and love that avoids any genuine human encounter or confrontation. One factor that encourages temporizing, avoidance, and accommodation is pastors' and church leaders' intimidating fear of rejection or criticism. Many seem preoccupied with "guarding the peace," maintaining peace at any price; their theme is "Don't rock the boat," a style that avoids conflicts for fear of "church fights," splits, or challenges to pastoral leadership.

THE URGENCY OF CHURCH RECONSIDER-ATION OF DISCIPLINE

Despite the relative lack of church discipline in most churches in the last fifty years, there is renewed interest in developing a proper understanding and practice of biblical church discipline. "The time is ripe" for the church to concentrate its attention on church discipline and our "disordered and confused world." The church needs "the rule of the Gospel," declared Heideman.[20]

The *Guinn* case heightened that interest and gave some visibility and focus to a brooding sense that perhaps there is something the church needs to reconsider. Various factors surely are at work in this reevaluation and reconsideration of church discipline. There is a sense of urgency in the restoration of a properly administered and thoroughly biblical redemptive discipline in the church. This conviction emerges from a number of bases.

DISCIPLINE IS A MATTER OF OBEDIENCE. For many, the question about church discipline is settled by the clear biblical mandate of Matthew 18. Whether or not the passage is seen as a specific formula, it clearly represents the teaching of our Lord concerning the church's authority and ministry of discipline. This teaching is reinforced by other New Testament passages and basic doctrines, as discussed in chapter three. Thus, church discipline is not an option, it is a command of Scripture.

DISCIPLINE PRESERVES THE INTEGRITY OF THE CHURCH.

We are set up for judgment and "judgment begins at the house of the Lord."

The "value vertigo" of modern society has invaded the church, and its integrity as a moral witness, moral teacher, and model has seriously eroded. Few would deny that the church today suffers from increased acculturation—a co-opting that has eroded its moral authority. It has so accommodated itself to the world that it often is unable to speak effectively even to its own members.

Yet the biblical faith is an ethical faith, and the covenant people of God are called to righteousness, holiness, and justice. The moral plasticity of modern culture and the church call out for discipline.

In such areas as family collapse, sexual immorality, materialism, and hedonism, the basic life of the church member seems little different than that of the nonchurch member. One recent Gallup poll concluded that while large numbers of Americans consider themselves "born again," there is little evidence that their moral behavior is substantially different from that of the surrounding culture.

We have lost the capacity to identify and name sin and speak decisively against it, and this has a debilitating effect on the spiritual vitality of the church. We are unable to identify moral boundaries and provide a protective universe in which Christian life may be lived.

The recovery of holiness demands church discipline; the encouragement and nurture of conscience demand church discipline; our sin demands discipline. We ought to insist on it for ourselves.

The theological integrity of the church is also at issue, and church discipline is necessary to preserve the character of the faith. This has been true from the earliest days; it is simply the right of self-preservation. No arguments about individual liberty, academic freedom, or popular ridicule of "heresy trials" and the like can negate the need for any group to preserve its doctrinal commitments. Unless all beliefs are negotiable and doctrine is purely a matter of personal persuasion, then discipline, both educative and corrective, is the necessary means of preserving the integrity of conviction in the church. While debates may rage about any particular theology and whether it is "good" or "bad," the right of a group—even its duty—to preserve the integrity of its central convictions, regardless of popular appeal, ought to be upheld. Muslims, fundamentalists, liberals, Hare Krishnas all have the right to a body of doctrine that is a test of fellowship and the right to censure or exclude those who affirm some other creed. The avoidance of syncretism and the clarity of faith demand church discipline.

DISCIPLINE PRESERVES THE WITNESS OF THE CHURCH.

A church without discipline is something less than a church and will never startle a jaded world. . . .[21]

The early church "turned the world upside down." In striking contrast, it has been suggested today that the modern world with its lack of conviction and commitment "can never generate enough movement in human society to get one handcart over the hills into the promised land."[22]

The global mission of the church is clear, a mission that encompasses not only evangelism but a prophetic moral voice. The world, we believe, is searching for models and signs of integrity, coherence, and wholeness, a "place to stand." Laury Eck suggested at a recent conference on church discipline that only a church that disciplines itself can speak such a prophetic word to the world.

Not only are we powerless in our own communities, but since we lack a coherent moral identity, we can hardly speak to the great moral issues of our culture—to racism, materialism, human rights, community values, science and technology, hunger, bioethics.

A church that wants to take stands in the world, to speak with some kind of authority, must be a church that takes stands in its own life. A church that speaks about the family crisis in the culture must examine its own elder board. A church that wants to take on "sin" in its personal and corporate dimensions in the world ought to address those issues in redemptive and healing ways in its own life.

DISCIPLINE ASSURES THAT THE CHURCH IS THE CHURCH! "Confusion concerning the nature of the church" is the basic cause for the wane in church discipline, argued Ben Patterson.[23] Probably no theological question touches the issue of church discipline more deeply than the nature of the church itself. We saw that in our brief survey of church history.

What is the church to be? What are its character, identity, marks, and mission? Until we know what the church is meant to be, we are powerless to address, theologically, the issue of church discipline. And yet we are faced not only with the longstanding, differing images of the church among denominations and traditions but also with those among local churches whose pastors and leaders do not necessarily understand or live within any tradition.

Is the church a leisure time activity, a sort of "hotel" where strangers occasionally gather on their travels through life,[24] or is it a unique community of persons who bind themselves both to one another and to the lordship of Christ as holy and redeemed people? Does its character imply commitments that are not options but must be kept, values that are to be cherished, conduct that is normative?

Surely Jacob Friesen is accurate when he observes that "biblical discipline is impossible in a group that calls itself a church but puts forth no sincere attempt to be a church."[25]

The existence of the "church" forces us to answer questions of church discipline no matter how much we may seek to ignore or postpone them. To claim to be a church begs the question, What does it mean to be a church?

What demands shall the church make upon her members . . . and by what methods shall she seek to secure conformity to her demands . . . ? Again, what is she to do if one . . . refuses to comply with her demands, or if the principles of conduct which he chooses . . . contradict those which she has evolved in her experience, or believes herself to hold as of divine institution? Is he to be left to go his own way, and to lead others with him? Or is the church to bring pressure to bear upon him, and if so at what point and in what measure?[26]

DISCIPLINE IS FOR MEANINGFUL CHURCH MEMBERSHIP.

Too often now when people join a church, they do so as a consumer. If they like the product, they stay; if they don't, they leave. They can no more imagine a church disciplining them then they could imagine a store that sells goods disciplining them. . . . We have a consumer mentality.[27]

Closely related to the nature of the church is the nature and meaning of membership. What does belonging mean? One observer noted that the requirements and expectations at any of the local civic or social clubs exceed the expectations of the church. Does it make any difference to identify with a body of believers and join the "ecclesia"?

Dean Kelley addressed the problem of "clubbiness of churches" that results in the notion that it would be churlish to refuse any of their friends' admittance. He pointed out that they have "confused friendship with the qualifications for membership. . . ."

Church discipline tells us that membership means something. It says that membership is a commitment. It teaches that membership is participation in a community with shared values and common, mutual obligations. It informs us of the obligation of membership to spiritual responsibility. Charles Deweese noted the absence of church discipline in the twentieth century and concluded the trend has "proved counterproductive to the growth of a regenerate church membership." We have reduced our "covenantal expectations" so that members have a "take it or leave it" mentality about membership. Our churches expect, and often get, little.

Perhaps we have been afraid to demand anything lest people would flee. The opposite conclusion was reached by Dean Kelley in his analysis of why conservative churches have grown while many mainstream Protestant groups have stayed even or declined. Kelley pointed to the relevance of the demands that the church puts on members. He concluded that the capacity of churches to give religious meaning to persons depends on the "demand they make upon their adherents and the degree to which that demand is met by commitment. Strong organizations are 'strict' and one which loses its strictness will lose its strength." The church seems to be governed by the law of entropy, leading to the deterioration of vitality.[28] Franklin Littell notes that historically churches have "halved the covenant for their children" till barely a sliver was left and the church was populated by "baptised pagans."[29]

But the question is not simply an issue of what will work. Strictness, stringency, and demand are as critical as the issues. Søren Kierkegaard spoke of "the severity which is inseparable from the seriousness of eternity."[30]

DISCIPLINE IS FOR OUR OWN SENSE OF IDENTITY.

One stakes one's life upon the particular yoke which one takes upon oneself. . . .[31]

Who are we? Social and psychological observers of our society note a confusion of identity in our world. We search for roots, for something that gives us a name, a character. Fred Cervin writes of the significance of discipline for the identity of the church and believer:

Discipline is the practical process through which both the church as a community and individuals within it work through the question of identity and boundary maintenance. It cannot be noncontroversial.[32]

A person's identity is known by defining the center and the boundaries of his life. For the Christian, both are inherent in the faith. Jesus Christ is the center, and the boundaries are set by the discipline of the church. "When the church is hesitant about either . . . it experiences an identity crisis."[33] If one cannot be "out," then one never knows whether one is really in. The community of faith is not a limitless community; "some people are within . . . and some are without."[34]

We believe the sense of identity that is encouraged and enforced by discipline is essential to our capacity to know who we are. It gives us our name. It is empowering rather than disabling. A strong identity will enable us to persevere. One observer noted that "the American church is no more ready to meet persecution than the German church was in 1933" and went on to suggest that the purpose of church discipline was not to censure infractions of nineteenth century middle-class values, but "to prepare the church for bitter, costly conflict with spiritual powers of wickedness."[35] We are unaccustomed to self-discipline and denial; we are possessive acquirers. Lacking character, we will likely be easy prey to the seducers whether they come with political, economic, or religious temptations.

DISCIPLINE CREATES A REDEMPTIVE COMMUNITY.

The church should be able to offer succor and healing to people in sin and in torment; and the church should be able to offer corrective discipline and restore sinners to a place of forgiveness.[36]

The church is the one place in society where we even dare to tell each other how we have sinned.[37]

"The church is the only army in the world that has the reputation for deserting its wounded," someone noted years ago. Proper church discipline, Don Baker insists, is a way of ensuring that we care for our wounded; we cannot ignore those who suffer quietly, however much they may find the healing treatment painful. Church discipline requires hanging on, persisting, a refusal to give up. Matthew 18 teaches a "rescue operation." The central purpose of church discipline is the restoration of the one who has sinned (1 Cor. 5:5; 1 Tim. 1:19, 20; 2 Thess. 3:13-15). We rob people of their right to be forgiven when we fail to confront them. We need not think of church discipline as a necessary evil.

"Church discipline . . . is not an embarrassment. . . . Unforgiven sin is the embarrassment."[38] When the church invites confession, it is offering a gift, not imposing a burden. Confession is a catharsis, a release essential for healing. To hide or internalize sin is to let it eat away at our integrity. There is a strong biblical character to public confession.

We desperately need that church discipline to provide healing, release, and forgiveness to the burdened and trapped members of our own communities. Without it we consign people to the privacy of their guilt. Discipline is one way the community is given identity and evidences its care. A society that no longer understands the meaning of discipline cannot understand the word of forgiveness, the teaching of righteousness, or the scandal of the cross.[39]

This redemptive work must be the work of the community, the mission of the gathered body of covenanters. The community invites and restores, provides strength and capacity. As Mowrer suggests, as long as a man lives in open touch with others he will vividly sense the consequences of right and wrong, and the community will provide the strength not to commit wrong.[40]

The biblical concept of the body assumes a mutuality and an accountability. If the church is to be revived, there must be a "true community of committed believers . . . and that will require precisely the discipline that is in such short supply."[41]

THE CHICKEN AND THE EGG!

There was "no room for error," observed Pastor Don Baker as he confronted the practice of discipline in his own church. How can discipline be healing and restorative? How can it be done right, be done biblically, be done redemptively? Where do we begin? If discipline requires a healthy community of faith in order to redeem, but to have such a community requires discipline, how do we escape a tragic loop?

Church discipline is not simply a matter of adopting bylaws and procedures and then going at it. It assumes a whole environment, a spiritual ecosystem in which discipline is not a destructive judgment that pushes people into conformity but rather a set of guidelines that call them to life.[42]

Discipline assumes the existence of a community—not simply an assemblage of persons—a community of people who know one another, who share their lives, who trust one another to treat them carefully. It is when the church is a family that discipline can possess the qualities of care.

In *Caring Enough to Confront* David Augsburger has suggested some of the conditions for effective "care-fronting"; caring before confronting, support before criticism, empathy before evaluation, trust before advice, affirmation before assessment.[43]

This mutuality of life has sustained a more effective church discipline in some religious communities, such as the Mennonites, than it has among independent, culturally adapted religious communities. Bonhoeffer spoke of this discipline rooted in commonness:

The basis upon which one Christian can speak to another is that each knows the other as a sinner, who, with all his human dignity, is lonely and lost if not given help. . . . Nothing could be more compassionate than the severe rebuke that calls a brother back from the path of sin.[44]

Discipline assumes mutual accountability. The whole church is always under discipline, including those who carry out discipline.[45] Discipline is not an *incident* in which some rare bylaw is invoked, but a *process* of mutual care. Discipline is not even an act, but a style of submitting ourselves one to another, calling each other to what we ought to be, not letting each other alone. It is, in a sense, a mutual choice we make to be "our brother's keeper." In such an environment, discipline in the sense of high visibility expulsions will be rare. Instead, we will share encouragement, admonitions, reminders, and "speaking the truth in love" that make us a community. "The way to not have to discipline is to discipline," observed one commentator.

NOTES

[1]Cited by Laury Eck, "The Recovery of the Ministry of Church Discipline," *The Recovery of the Ministry of Church Discipline* (Albuquerque, N.M.: Christian Conciliation Services, 1982). Sound cassette.

[2]Harry G. Coiner, "Living toward One Another with the Word of God: A Study of Mutual Care and Discipline in the Church," *Concordia Theological Monthly*, Oct. 1965, 613.

[3]Marlin Jeschke, "Toward an Evangelical Conception of Corrective Church Discipline" (Ph.D. diss., Northwestern University, 1965), 237.

[4]Emil Brunner, *The Divine Imperative* (Philadelphia: Westminster Press, 1947), 558, 559, cited by Marlin Jeschke, *Discipling the Brother* (Scottdale, Pa.: Herald Press, 1972), 37.

[5]Henry IV, master of Germany after 1075, had, along with his nobles and bishops, challenged the authority of the pope in 1076, even fiercely denouncing him. Gregory VII (Hildebrand), who was a supreme advocate of papal power, responded with a papal decree excommunicating Henry IV, declaring that his subjects no longer owed any duties to the pope. Church historian Williston Walker calls it the "boldest assertion of papal authority that ever has been made." Henry replied, calling Hildebrand "now no pope, but a false monk." But Henry's political fortunes deteriorated, and the nobles insisted he obtain release from the excommunication or he would be dethroned. Facing the loss of the throne, Henry traveled to meet Hildebrand in northern Italy while the pope was

on his way to Germany for a meeting at Augsburg. Hildebrand had taken refuge in a castle to which for three successive days Henry came barefoot as a penitent, and finally Gregory relented and released Henry from the excommunication. See Williston Walker, *A History of the Christian Church* (New York: Scribner's Sons, 1959), 208-211.

[6]Roberta Green, "Church Discipline: Can Courts Pass Judgment?" *The Register*, 29 Apr. 1984, A1, A18, 19.

[7]See *Webster's Ninth New Collegiate Dictionary* (Springfield, Mass.: Merriam-Webster Inc., 1983) s.v., "discipline."

[8]Cited in *Studies in Church Discipline*, ed. Maynard Shelley (Newton, Kans.: Faith & Life, 1958), 56.

[9]The definition in *The New Schaff-Herzog Encyclopedia of Religion*, ed. D. M. Jackson (Grand Rapids: Baker Book House, 1950) III:8, emphasizes this corrective aspect: "Church discipline is a means of securing and maintaining the spiritual priority of the Christian church. This exercise arises from the fact that the church is a human institution, the members of which are subject to the limitations and weaknesses of humanity. The Christian congregation, therefore, like every other community, needs a means of self-protection in order to suppress or eliminate whatever might impair or destroy its life."

[10]James Travis, "Discipline in the New Testament," *Pastoral Psychology*, Dec. 1965, 21.

[11]Laury Eck, "Restoring the Ministry of Church Discipline," *The Recovery of the Ministry of Church Discipline* (Albuquerque, N.M.: Christian Conciliation Services, 1982). Sound cassette.

[12]See Kenneth E. Kirk, *The Vision of God* (London: Longmans, Green, & Co., 1931), 132ff., for an excellent section on the major difficulties with a formalistic code. Kirk discusses the emphasis on correct behavior rather than motive, the tendency to substitute "punctiliousness for piety," which makes the ideal of self-forgetfulness impossible, and the dangers of moral complacency and inviting the despair that comes from scrupulosity (e.g., Romans 7).

[13]Marvin Ewert, "Personality and Discipline," in Maynard Shelley, ed., *Studies in Church Discipline* (Newton, Kans.: Faith & Life, 1958), 99.

[14]Of course these "abuses" are theologically assessed and traditions will view some practices quite differently,

e.g., the role of the congregation versus church leaders such as elders, pastors, and bishops.

[15]Cited by Jeschke, *Discipling the Brother,* 14 (emphasis added).

[16]Cited by Samuel Southard, "Pastoral Judgment," *Pastoral Psychology,* Dec. 1965, 16.

[17]Gregory the Great, *Pastoral Care,* trans. Henry Davis (Westminster, Md.: Newman Press, 1950).

[18]Donald P. Smith, *Clergy in the Crossfire* (Philadelphia: Westminster Press, 1973).

[19]Don Baker, *Beyond Forgiveness: The Healing Touch of Church Discipline* (Portland, Oreg.: Multnomah Press, 1984), 78. Of course, effective leadership is more than giving commands, and in a Christian tradition there is a reversal of roles in genuine leadership, so that the leader becomes the servant. Many Christians have been impressed with Robert Greenleaf's *Servant Leadership* (New York: Paulist Press, 1977) as a reflection of important insights about true servanthood in contemporary public and private life.

[20]Eugene P. Heideman, "The Church and Christian Discipline," *Reformed Review,* Mar. 1963, 29.

[21]John White, *Eros Defiled* (Downers Grove, Ill.: InterVarsity Press, 1977), 158.

[22]Dean Kelley, *Why the Conservative Churches Are Growing* (New York: Harper & Row, 1972), 53.

[23]Ben Patterson, "Discipline: The Backbone of the Church," *Leadership,* Winter 1983, 109.

[24]"Here is not a hotel theory of church discipline such as prevails too often in modern times, or an ark theory such as Cyprian anciently taught. . . . In a hotel, people of all types sit down for a brief time at the table and then part, knowing and caring little about one another. In the ark, there were all kinds of animals, the ferocious lion with the innocent lamb and all were saved alike by being in the ark. . . . But in a true church every member is vitally responsible for the character of the group as a whole. . . ." John W. Shepard, *The Christ of the Gospels: An Exegetical Study* (Grand Rapids, Mich.: Eerdmans, 1954), 335 (commenting on Matthew 18).

[25]Jacob Friesen, "Where Do We Begin?" in Maynard Shelley, ed., *Studies in Church Discipline* (Newton, Kans.: Faith & Life, 1958), 129.

[26]Kirk, 4.

[27]Cited by Laury Eck, "The Recovery of the Ministry of Church Discipline," *The Recovery of the Ministry of Church Discipline* (Albuquerque, N.M.: Christian Conciliation Services, 1982). Sound cassette.

[28]Kelley, 96.

[29]Ibid., 110. Franklin Littell notes the danger in stringency, which is spontaneous in an early movement, quickly degenerating into a formalized, external imitation that is counterfeit. The result is "fossilized."

[30]Søren Kierkegaard, *Attack on Christendom* (Boston: Beacon Books, 1956), 123.

[31]Jay C. Rochelle, "Probings Toward Ecclesial Discipline in a Pluralistic Age," *Currents in Theology and Mission,* Aug. 1983, 243.

[32]Fred Cervin, "A Dream of Order: Notes on Church Discipline," *The Covenant Quarterly,* Aug. 1977, 6.

[33]Eugene P. Heideman, "Discipline and Identity," *Reformed Review,* Fall 1981, 17.

[34]Rochelle, 224.

[35]Cervin, 9.

[36]White, 151.

[37]Lewis S. Mudge, *In His Service* (Philadelphia: Westminster Press, 1959), 130.

[38]Jeschke, "Church Discipline," 238.

[39]Heideman, "Christian Discipline," *Reformed Review,* Mar. 1963, 29.

[40]O. H. Mowrer, *The Crisis in Psychiatry and Religion* (Princeton, N.J.: D. Van Nostrand, 1961), 216.

[41]Harold O. J. Brown, "The Role of Discipline in the Church," *Covenant Quarterly,* Aug. 1983, 52.

[42]Cervin, "A Dream of Order," 6.

[43]David Augsburger, *Caring Enough to Confront* (Glendale, Calif.: Regal Books, 1980), 52.

[44]Dietrich Bonhoeffer, *Life Together* (New York: Harper & Row, 1976), 105, 106.

[45]Marvin Ewert, "Personality and Discipline," in Maynard Shelley, ed., *Studies in Church Discipline* (Newton, Kans.: Faith & Life, 1958), 97-104.

5

ENTER THE SHERIFF

Whatever the theological base for church discipline, the *Guinn* case and its progeny have raised new and troubling questions. Professor James McGoldrick[1] has suggested that the *Guinn* decision, if it stands upon appeal, would constitute one of the most significant threats to the free exercise of religion in America's history.

What legal liabilities can a church incur when it follows what it believes is a biblical pattern of church discipline? Are there ways to minimize these risks? Is the church going to be vulnerable to "spite" lawsuits brought by disgruntled former members? Will churches need to hire lawyers every time they admonish or discipline members?

These are legitimate concerns. At the philosophical level there is proper anxiety about judicial intrusion into the life of the church. At the immediate local and pragmatic levels, the church wishes to be fully faithful to Scripture yet not to incur unnecessary liability or waste its valuable time and resources in protracted legal disputes. Pastor and church leaders quite legitimately seek guidance in this confusing area. Several questions have emerged: What is the legal basis for *Guinn* and similar claims? On what grounds may the church and its leaders be sued? And what are the consequences for the church, its pastor, and its governing board? What are the risks, and how may they be minimized without sacrificing principle? How can the potentially dangerous intrusions into affairs of doctrine and internal church life be effectively resisted by sound legal principles and carefully developed church procedures?

In this section we shall provide an overview of the legal issues in these church discipline cases, including:

1. What are basic rights of associations such as churches to control their own affairs? And what are the limits on these rights?

2. What are the traditional claims made in church discipline cases? What types of cases have been successfully brought against churches in connection with church discipline practices, and how may they be avoided?

3. What are the new questions and legal tactics raised by the *Guinn* decision, and how do they affect church practices and liabilities?

4. What are the basic "defenses" of churches against such legal actions?

As surprising and unusual as the *Guinn* case may appear, legal issues have frequently emerged concerning the actions of churches, including their exercise of church discipline. In an earlier period when churches were more willing to discipline and even expel members, aggrieved parties frequently sought relief from the courts. Such attempts ran immediately into two basic legal obstacles: the protection of the rights of association, and the protection of religious liberty.

RIGHTS OF ASSOCIATION

Americans have always been joiners, and though the Constitution does not specifically speak about a right to form an association, its protections of speech and assembly have been found to imply such a right. In 1963 the Supreme Court interpreted the First Amendment to protect the freedom of association.

There is no longer any doubt the First and Fourteenth Amendments protect certain forms of orderly group activity. Thus, we have affirmed the right to engage in association for the advancement of beliefs and ideals.[2]

A few years later in *Griswold v. Connecticut* the Court spelled out the scope of that freedom.

The right of "association" like the right of "belief" is more than the right to attend a meeting; it includes the right to express one's attitudes or philosophies by membership in a group or by affiliation with it or by other lawful means; association in that context is a form of expression or opinion; and while it is not expressly included in the First Amendment its existence is necessary in making express guarantees fully meaningful.[3]

Thus, the Constitution protects the rights of individuals not simply to engage in free speech but to act in concert with others of like mind. The effect is to provide First Amendment rights not simply to individuals, but to groups as well and thus to insulate their activities from unreasonable governmental intrusion.

Such rights, being grounded in fundamental constitutional liberties, are entitled to strong protection against infringement. Only interests of a very high order, called "compelling interests," can justify the state's intrusion on a fundamental liberty. The Supreme Court made this point about rights of association quite clearly in 1958 when it declared that "state action which may have

the effect of curtailing the freedom to association is subject to the closest scrutiny."[4]

Issues about rights to control membership
in churches are in part controlled by the law
concerning the rights of association and individual members rights. While some additional protections may well be provided by the
First Amendment's religion clauses, much of
the liberty of the church also derives from
rights of association.

THE RIGHT TO ESTABLISH ITS OWN BINDING GOVER-
NANCE.

[It is] well established that a voluntary association may, without direction or interference by
the courts, draw up for its own government and
adopt rules, regulations, and bylaws which will
be controlling as to all questions of discipline,
doctrine, or internal policy; and its right to interpret and administer such rules and regulations is
as sacred as its right to make them.[5]

Associations have a degree of self-govern-
ment, an internal legislative power.[6] This
power is not unlimited, but so long as the
regulations of the association are not immoral, unreasonable, illegal, or in violation of a
strong public policy, they will be held valid
and binding on all members. This is true
even if the effect of these rules is to limit
freedom they might otherwise have had
were it not for their voluntary membership.

THE "RULES" OF THE ASSOCIATION ARE BINDING ON
ALL ITS MEMBERS. Not only may associations
determine their own rules, but those rules
are binding on all members. Since the association is voluntary, courts will normally view
these rules and expectations as binding on
all the members who have notice of them.
Usually if such rules are contained in the bylaws, courts will hold that all members legally had notice and are deemed to have

consented to them, and cannot, therefore, be heard to object to their enforcement.[7]

The basic perspective here is one of contract law; that is, members of a voluntary association have agreed among each other, have made a bargain regarding certain rules, procedures, and expectations, and cannot later complain about the bargain they struck. If persons do not wish to participate under certain rules they either may decline to join or withdraw. The ability to enforce rules is derived from the consent of the persons who have freely associated themselves together under these rules.

THE RIGHT TO ESTABLISH CONDITIONS FOR MEMBERSHIP. This right to establish the internal structure of a voluntary association extends to the conditions of membership including eligibility and qualifications. Associations may choose to impose whatever terms they want as long as they are not contrary to law.[8] The granting or denial of membership in a voluntary organization is "within the complete control of the association, and the courts cannot compel the admission of an individual into such an association." Nor may one excluded from membership sue for damages for such exclusion, even where the exclusion may have been motivated by malice.[9]

This rule does not apply where the association is not really voluntary, as in an association in which membership is required for the practice of a profession or the character of the association takes it beyond the private associational arena. At times associational rights will compete with other rights. This was illustrated in a well-publicized 1985 case involving the Jaycees organization. The Supreme Court balanced the Jaycees' associational rights to control admission to membership against the state interest in preventing sex discrimination. The Court reviewed the purposes of the Jaycees organization, decided there was no relationship between the "men only" policy and those purposes, and held that under those circumstances the absolute exclusion of women members was impermissible.[10]

THE RIGHT TO DETERMINE THE BASIS AND PROCEDURES FOR DISCIPLINARY PRACTICES WITHIN THE ASSOCIATION. An association must have the "power to relieve itself of its discordant members" so that harmony may prevail. Thus an association has the right to "establish bylaws providing for the expulsion of members transgressing their reasonable provisions."[11]

The members of an association may prescribe rules of conduct for themselves during their membership, with penalties for their violation, and a tribunal and mode in which the offenses shall be determined and the penalty enforced.[12]

When decisions are made under such rules by the appropriate tribunal set up by the association, the decisions with respect to internal disciplinary affairs traditionally are not reviewed except in case of "fraud, illegality, collusion or arbitrariness." Otherwise, the decisions are conclusive.[13]

The powers of an association to provide for suspension or expulsion of members have usually been perceived as inherent in the association itself, what some courts have called the "police power of an organization." One court referred to this right to expel members as rooted in "a basic law of self-preservation."

These general principles of the rights of associations apply to religious societies as well. Churches may promulgate rules that regulate the expulsion of members and such rules are binding on all of its members.[14] The Supreme Court in *Bouldin v. Alexander* declared that "we have no power to revise or question ordinary acts of church discipline, or of exclusion from membership."[15]

In addition to protecting the rights of associations, judicial review of the decisions and acts of churches is limited by constitutional protections of religious liberty.

In numerous cases courts have refrained from interference with church decisions, stressing the general principles of religious liberty and the specific restraints of separation of church and state.[16] The Supreme Court in 1872 set the tone when it declared:

Whenever the questions of discipline, or of faith, or ecclesiastical rule, custom or law have been decided by the highest of these church judicatories to which the matter has been carried, the legal tribunals must accept these decisions as final, and binding on them. . . . The right to organize voluntary religious associations . . . and to create tribunals for the decision of controverted questions of faith within the association, and for the ecclesiastical government of all the individual members . . . is unquestioned. *All who unite themselves to such a body do so with an implied consent to its government, and are bound to submit to it.* But it would be a vain consent and would lead to the total subversion of such religious bodies, if anyone aggrieved by one of their decisions could appeal to the secular courts and have them reversed. It is of the essence of these religious unions, and of their right to establish tribunals . . . that those decisions should be binding in all cases of ecclesiastical cognizance, subject only to such appeals as the organism itself provides for.[17]

These associational rights of churches specifically embrace many of the issues concerning the rights of churches in disciplining members. In *Guinn,* for example, the church as an association was clearly within its rights to identify the bases of membership and establish means and tribunals for the exercise of associational discipline. This was part of its internal police power and a necessary part of its self-preservation. Its report to the church and sister churches and its advice to members about their response to the disciplined and excluded member were also part of its policing of internal affairs.

The rules and conditions of membership may be set by the church and need not reflect cultural judgments and values. In fact, one aspect of associational protections is to assure the vitality of unique institutions that contribute to our pluralism. Environmentalists form associations whose members are vigorously committed to protecting the environment, and they may quite appropriately and necessarily preserve those values by rules for membership that exclude or expel willful polluters. Feminist groups similarly have the right to expect members to conform their conduct to the values of their group. So it is with the church. The church's role as a faith community and a prophetic witness to its society, its capacity for moral life and influence, is seriously weakened whenever individuals or society through public law compel it to compromise its norms or to conform to prevailing "public policies."

The rights of association are important to preserve the rights of groups such as churches to identify their values and purposes and to gather a group of persons who will live and act consistently with those. Church discipline arises from such a commitment by the body, with some special central convictions.

Such strong commitments in the area of associational rights have not prevented legal challenges to church disciplinary proceedings.

These claims usually involve one or both of two elements: (1) charges that the expulsion was *procedurally improper* and hence invalid or (2) a *substantive* claim that some personal or property right was violated and that the plaintiff is entitled to money damages for that violation. This second category of actions usually involves tort claims of one variety or another. Traditionally the claim most often raised is *defamation* by libel or slander. The *Guinn* case and its copycat suits reflect, however, new and troublesome bases—allegations of *invasion of privacy* and *infliction of emotional distress.*

In the next chapters we will review these bases for church liability and then consider the larger constitutional defense of the religious liberty clause of the Constitution. But it is first essential to understand the potential claims that churches have acted improperly by violating their own *procedures.*

PLAYING BY THE RULES

While associational rights ought to be strong grounds for barring court interference with church decisions about internal matters including church disciplinary actions, that has not precluded court battles. One of the major grounds for challenging dismissals from membership has been a challenge not to the *right* of the association to control its membership but rather a challenge to the means or *process* the association used. These may be thought of as *procedural* claims. It is a way of saying: "You had a right to dismiss members, but not to do it the way you did."

These claims based on procedural questions continue to be problems for churches that ignore their own bylaws in carrying out all types of activities from buying property to disciplining church members. The tragic results include lost time, lost resources, and dissension. Perhaps the most frequent issue involving members' claims against churches is over their procedures, and certainly it is one of the challenges most likely to succeed. In fact, in many cases challenges on procedural grounds are the only ways in which the actual action of the church may be held to be void and members reinstated.[1⁹]

The basic nature of a procedural claim is to allege that something was wrong with the procedures followed by the church in taking its action, that they were in some way irregular, improper proceedings. These questions of procedure in a church discipline case may deal with whether the proper notice was given to the person(s) concerning the charges or concerning meetings to consider charges, whether there was an opportunity for a hearing, or whether the proper body (e.g., deacons, elders, congregation) within the church made the decision.

In re Baptist Church is a classic church fight, including the dismissal of the pastor and removal of certain members from leadership positions. Each side held meetings purporting to reverse what the other "faction" had done (the court referred to the factions as the pro-pastor and the anti-pastor faction). The court assessed which church meetings were properly held and what constituted "adequate notice" to members. It then set forth the limited basis for a procedural appeal, and concluded:

Spiritualities are beyond the reach of temporal courts, and a pastor may be deposed by a majority of the members at a congregational meeting at any time, so far as the civil courts are concerned, subject only to the inquiry by the courts as to whether the church, or its appointed tribunal, has proceeded according to the law of the church.[19]

The most usual form of such a challenge is really a reaffirmation of associational rights, because at the heart of such a claim is the allegation that the association has not followed its rules and procedures. The argument is that the association may have the right to make its own rules, but it must then abide by them. On such grounds a number of complaints have been raised including the following as examples.

DID THE PROPER AUTHORITY DECIDE THE ISSUE? Challenges based on the expelling person's or group's lack of authority under the bylaws have been successful in a number of cases, such as where the pastor alone dismissed a member in a congregational church,[20] where a church appellate tribunal reviewing a decision was improperly constituted,[21] where the expulsion was by an unauthorized committee revising the church constitution,[22] and where unauthorized persons usurped control of the church tribunal.[23]

WERE SPECIFIC PROCEDURES OBSERVED? Other occasionally successful challenges to church decisions have been where the specific church steps or procedures, such as those regarding notice of meetings, have not been followed. For example, in the 1949 case *David v. Carter,* the court found a "radical departure from accepted customs and rules of organization" when it reviewed the expulsion of a member who had no previous notice of the time, place, or purpose of the meeting.[24]

In *Taylor v. Jackson* the court reversed several expulsions because the notice was insufficient and a copy of charges was not properly served as required by the rules of the denomination.[25] In *Longmeyer v. Payne* the court reversed expulsions where the plaintiffs were given no notice or opportunity to be heard, contrary to the church's own rules.[26] A final illustration is *Randolph v.*

First Baptist Church where an expulsion was held invalid. The pastor announced a meeting to deal with members who had opposed the advancement of the church's program but failed to note that the plaintiff Randolph was referred to but had not been given notice of the charges against her before the trial. The court observed that although a church is autonomous and the minority must submit to the majority, it does not follow that the church can expel members with utter disregard of constitutional provisions regarding expulsion of members.[27]

In situations such as these, which are based on the church's violation of its own procedures as set forth in its governing documents, it is not unusual for the courts to engage in a limited review of the church's actions and set aside those that were in violation of its own commitments. Courts do have jurisdiction to determine "whether the expelling organization acted in accordance with its own regulations."[28]

Courts are nonetheless traditionally reluctant to interfere even when there are irregularities. In *Mt. Olive Primitive Baptist Church v. Patrick* the Alabama Supreme Court refused to intervene in a dismissal of members without notice, arguing that to do so would be "treading on dangerous ground and invading a sanctuary." It concluded that

the church being independent, and not subject to higher powers, and being a law unto itself for its own procedures in religious matters, what it did towards the expulsion of petitioner was not unlawful, even if it was not politic and wise.[29]

WERE THE PROCEDURES UNFAIR? Occasionally, where the church has no formal procedures set forth or where they are minimal, disgruntled parties who have been expelled have alleged that the procedures were improper because of their basic unfairness, or that they violated "natural justice." Here, the court is asked to examine not simply whether the procedures followed were consistent with the church's own procedural rules, but whether in the absence of sufficient safeguards the procedures were unfair as a matter of law.

In *Rock Dell N. Evangelical Lutheran Church v. Mommsen* the court held that an expulsion without any notice, any formal charges being brought, or any opportunity to be heard was void even though there was no requirement for such in the church's own rules.[30] Similar decisions based on concepts of natural justice have been handed down in other jurisdictions. These courts speak of a presumption of such requirements.[31] In a number of Baptist church cases, courts have even looked outside the local church to discover Baptist procedural expectations. A number have relied on Hiscox's "Directory for Baptist Churches" as a generally acceptable guide to Baptist polity and practice, suggesting that Baptist procedures require that the accused be furnished with a copy of the charges, notice of the time and place of the trial, and be given ample opportunity to present a defense.[32]

Another aspect of natural justice is whether or not an expulsion may be challenged on grounds of lack of good faith. One court affirmed its general lack of authority to review an expulsion "except to ascertain . . . whether or not it was in good faith."[33] But other courts have rejected any "good faith" exception, suggesting they have no jurisdiction to inquire into motives.[34] Still other courts have specifically declined to impose any natural justice principles.[35]

A few cases alleged that the church's bylaws violated principles of fairness. Under general associational law, corporate bylaws of religious bodies will control unless they are found to be "unreasonable, unadapted to the corporate purpose, or contrary or inconsistent with the laws of the state. . . ."[36]

It is rare for church bylaws provisions to be successfully challenged. Courts have upheld provisions such as those requiring church attendance, pew ownership, and financial support. But one court did strike down a provision for automatic expulsion of persons in arrears in payments on the grounds that if a hearing had been provided, the fact of the arrears might have been challenged.[37]

It is important to note that courts are reluctant to inquire too deeply into procedural aspects of associational rights when churches are involved because constitutional protections of religion complicate any judicial review. The Supreme Court in the *Watson* case, already noted, indicated it was nervous about reviewing such questions because of the risk of becoming involved in examining "with minuteness and care" the usages, customs, laws, and organizations of religious denominations and thus interfering with the rights and processes of such bodies in "construing their own church laws." Some major reasons for this reticence are the Constitutional guarantees in the First Amendment, which we will examine later.

One further basis for such a reluctance to intervene is the fact that courts lack special knowledge of ecclesiastical matters; the ecclesiastical bodies themselves are the "best judges of their own law."[38]

A few courts have even suggested that they would not review a church decision about membership on any grounds. In early cases, courts often applied a rule that prevented review of any expulsion unless there was "some property or civil right" involved.[39] Since most courts did not find a "right" in mere membership, they declined to interfere. Such a rule led to a "hands off" posture, including some unusual decisions, such as in *Jenkins v. New Shiloh Baptist Church.* In *New Shiloh,* the church's constitution and *Book of Discipline* established various rules for church discipline actions. Yet the church ignored these provisions, including a requirement of an initial review of any contemplated discipline by pastors and deacons. There was a lack of notice of pending expulsion action at a called meeting, a lack of opportunity for plaintiff to be heard, and even nonmembers were allowed to vote —all against the church's own rules. Yet the court still declined to interfere.[40]

CONCLUSION

Keep in mind two items about procedural problems.

First, the traditional and general rule is that the expulsion of members according to the powers and procedures set forth in the church's governing documents is valid and is not subject to review by courts. Disciplinary proceedings consonant with the bylaws and established procedures of the church are unlikely to be successfully challenged on procedural grounds in a secular court. When the courts do take note of improper procedures, the church cannot complain because it is expected to follow its own agreements.

In cases where both sides claim the property, each expelling the other, the court *must* intervene and inquire into proper procedures.

Second, the impact of judicial interventions on procedural grounds usually is not significant. While the intervention may reinstate the members (not to mention the waste of the church's resources), what often follows is that the church simply repeats the process again, paying careful attention to the proper procedures.

Courts may overturn church actions based on improper procedures. Fortunately in this area the church largely can control its own destiny. The church must pay proper attention to the way it conducts its affairs, observing its own commitments as to process and seeking to be just and fair to all parties.

NOTES

[1] Associate Dean and Professor of Constitutional Law, Pepperdine University College of Law.

[2] *NAACP v. Button*, 371 U.S. 415, 430 (1963). The Supreme Court has specifically extended associational rights to such groups as labor organizations, political parties, commercial organizations, and, in *Kedroff v. St. Nicholas Cathedral of Russian Orthodox Church*, 344 U.S. 94 (1952), religious bodies.

[3] *Griswold v. Connecticut*, 381 U.S. 479, 1483 (1964).

[4] *NAACP v. Alabama*, 357 U.S. 449, 461 (1958).

[5] Am. Jur. 2d *Associations and Clubs* § 5 (1963).

[6] This is true whether or not the association is incorporated.

[7] Subject to a few limits in specialized cases, this is true even though the rules and regulations may have changed through proper organizational decisions since membership commenced, and even if the changes were voted against by one who objects.

[8] Am. Jr. 2d § 19.

[9] See 6 Am. Jur. 2d § 18 citing *State* ex rel. *Baumhoff v. Taxpayer's League*, 875 S.W.2d 207 (Mo. App. 1935); *Trauwien v. Harbourt*, 123 A.2d 30 (N.J. 1956).

[10] *Roberts v. United States Jaycees*, 104 S. Ct. 3244 (1983).

[11] See *Del Ponte v. Societa Italiana*, 27 R.I. 1, 60 A. 237 (1905).

[12] 6 Am. Jur. 2d § 20.

[13] 6 Am. Jur. 2d § 27.

75788

[14]6 Am. Jur. 2d §12, citing *Jones v. State*, 28 Neb. 495, 44 N.W. 658 (1963).

[15]*Bouldin v. Alexander*, 15 Wall. 131, 82 U.S. 131 (1832).

[16]For a list of such cases in various jurisdictions see Annot., "Suspension or Expulsion from a Religious Society," 20 A.L.R.2d §§ 5, 6 (1965).

[17]*Watson v. Jones*, 13 Wall. 679, 20 L. Ed. 666 (1872) (emphasis added).

[18]For a general overview of issues and cases associated with challenges to expulsions see Annot., "Suspension or expulsion from a church or religious society and the remedies therefore," 20 A.L.R.2d, 418ff. (1965) and "Religious Societies," 66 Am. Jur. 2d, § 12, 766 (1973).

[19]*In re Baptist Church*, 186 So. 2d 102, 106 (Ala. 1966).

[20]*Burke v. Roper*, 79 Ala. 138 (1885).

[21]*Hatfield v. De Long*, 156 Ind. 207, 59 N.E. 483 (1901).

[22]*Keith v. Howard*, 24 Pick. 292 (Mass. 1836).

[23]*Briscoe v. Williams*, 192 S.W.2d 643 (Mo. App. 1946), declared that an expelled member "has a right to be heard . . . on the question whether unauthorized persons have usurped control of the church tribunal."

[24]*David v. Carter*, 222 S.W.2d 900 (Tex. Civ. App. 1949).

[25]*Taylor v. Jackson*, 273 F. 345 (D.C. 1921) (Baptist church).

[26]*Longmeyer v. Payne*, 205 S.W.2d 263 (Mo. App. 1947).

[27]*Randolph v. First Baptist Church*, 53 Ohio Op. 2d 288, 120 N.E.2d 485 (1954).

[28]*Brown v. Mt. Olive Baptist Church*, 255 Iowa 857, 124 N.W.2d 445 (1963).

[29]*Mt. Olive Primitive Baptist Church v. Patrick*, 42 So. 2d 617 (1949), reprinted in 20 A.L.R.2d 417 at 420.

[30]*Rock Dell N. Evangelical Lutheran Church v. Mommsen*, 174 Minn. 207, 219 N.W. 88 (1928).

[31]For example, in *Hughes v. North Clinton Baptist Church*, 75 N.J.L. 167, 67 A. 66 (1907) the court voided a dismissal without cause, charges, or opportunity to be heard. In *In re Koch*, 257 N.Y. 318, 178 N.E. 545, the court held a dismissal void where there was no adequate notice or opportunity to be heard.

[32]See a more current and abbreviated edition of Hiscox: Edward T. Hiscox, *The Hiscox Guide for Baptist Churches* (Valley Forge, Pa.: Judson Press, 1964). Chap-

ter 8 deals with church discipline. Several notes at the conclusion of the chapter deal with procedures. Note 1: "Any one tried by a church should be allowed every opportunity, both as to time, place, and circumstances, to vindicate himself. . . ."

[33]*Brown v. Harris County Medical Society*, 194 S.W. 1179 (Tex. Civ. App. 1917); the court relied on earlier cases involving associational rights, including religious groups.

[34]*Clapp v. Krug*, 232 Ky. 303, 22 S.W.2d 1025 (1929).

[35]Examples of courts specifically indicating they would not assess whether an expulsion was violative of "natural justice" are *Partin v. Tucker*, 126 Fla. 817, 172 So. 89 (1937) (compare, however, later Florida decision in *First Free Will Baptist Church, Inc. v. Franklin*, 148 Fla. 277, 4 So. 2d 390 [1941] implying that a review for "arbitrariness" might be considered); and *Minton v. Leavell*, 297 S.W. 615 (Tex. Civ. App. 1927).

[36]*Fairchild v. Tillotson*, 118 Misc. 689, 195 N.Y.S. 39 (1922) (involving incorporated Christian Science church).

[37]See 20 A.L.R.2d § 9 (462, 463).

[38]Cases making this point are numerous. See, for example, *Morris Street Baptist Church v. Dart*, 67 S.C. 338, 45 S.E. 753, 100 Am. St. Rep. 727 (1903).

[39]Courts are divided on whether membership itself is such a right. The majority rule historically has seemed to be that it is not, though Texas and Nebraska courts have found that it is at least a "valuable right" and have intervened on that basis. Where, of course, the case also raises issues of rights or property or income, the "property or civil right" requirement is easily met.

[40]*Jenkins v. New Shiloh Baptist Church*, 189 Md. 512, 56, A.2d 788 (1948). Similarly in *Murr v. Maxwell*, 232 S.W.2d 219 (Mo. App. 1950) the court refused to intervene in spite of allegations that procedures for calling proper business meetings were not followed, no testimony was received, and Matthew 18 was not observed.

6 KEEPING SECRETS

If you can't trust your pastor to keep a secret, who can you trust?

Suppose you went to your pastor and confessed a continuing problem of shoplifting or adultery. You sought his prayers and counsel. You prayed with him for God's forgiveness and strength to renew your life. But alas, the problem continued; you tired of the pastor's confrontation and spoke no further with him about it. Then suppose you found out he had told the deacons about your problem. Or imagine he told you that unless you changed your conduct, he would "tell it to the church." What would your reaction be?

What if you were the pastor? What would you do? Would you advise other church leaders and follow step two of Matthew 18? Would you eventually "tell it to the church"? Or is the information confidential?

Or suppose the counseling ministry of your church is ministering to a church member who acknowledges a drug problem that is affecting her marriage and work. She has been nominated by the church for a position of leadership. As a counselor, what should you do with this information—morally, biblically, legally?

Such situations pose difficult ethical, pastoral, and legal problems because of the issue of confidentiality.

Most of us expect that if we acknowledge a transgression or identify a problem to our pastor it is personal and not intended to be shared with others. Indeed, most of us would be quite surprised and angry to hear our "story" become the sermon illustration on Sunday or used as a church discipline "case" for the elders. When we seek spiritual help with a problem we do not expect it to become public information. Yet when the counseling is proving ineffective and the ongoing conduct is serious and destructive, there are biblical expectations that seem to run against absolute secrecy. From a purely spiritual perspective, what we wish to keep hidden and secret may need to be brought into the light.

Church discipline "cases" frequently raise claims that the church discipline process violated an expectation of confidentiality when the information revealed in counseling or confession was then divulged to church leaders.

Charles Roberson in his suit against the Evangelical Orthodox Church alleged that the revelations to the defendant Weldon Hardenbrook were "a penitential communication" made "as a penitent to his clergyman." He claimed he asked the pastor and others "to keep his communication confidential," but that in spite of this the defendants "told numerous other persons." These acts were, the complaint alleged, a "breach of fiduciary duty"—a duty to "the highest standard of trust, confidence and fair dealing."

Similarly, in John Kelly's suit against the Christian Community Church and Dr. Donald Phillips, the complaint alleged that Kelly had secured Phillips's services as a counselor and "in the course of treament [Kelly] disclosed confidential . . . details of his sexual and marital life" and that Dr. Phillips then "released confidential information" to the church board of elders. These acts of Phillips were, it is argued, "negligent, careless, reckless and/or in derogation of his professional duties."

To some extent these claims sound very much like the "invasion of privacy" issue, but though the concern about revealing "private" facts is the same, the legal basis is different. Here the allegation is not an invasion of privacy, but a claim that the pastor or counselor was negligent. The negligence arises from an implied agreement between the parties, based on their relationship, that this information would not be shared, that it was an agreement to keep matters confidential. It is further argued that the role of pastor or counselor carries with it a professional duty to keep such communications confidential.

The legal argument is that the recipient of the communication (the pastor, for example) was under a legal duty not to disclose what he had been told in confidence. When he reveals the information, he violates a trust, breaching his duty to preserve the confidences of the counseling process.

This creates tension. If the church is to have effective counseling, there must be strong elements of trust and reliance that the information shared will be held in confidence. If there is no expectation of confidentiality, few will venture to reveal embarrassing personal facts or acknowledge their shortcomings. People seek counseling not for publicity but for help.

Yet it is in such pastoral conversation, whether in formal counseling or not, that pastors and counselors may obtain information about conduct that, if not changed, would call for further church efforts to encourage repentance and restoration. These efforts could include discipline. How can these seemingly contradictory expectations be dealt with?

Of course, there is no conflict when the confiding party is genuinely repentant and seeking God's renewal, even if in a stumbling, slow, and often inadequate way. Here the confidence is respected in keeping with biblical principles as well as any personal or professional expectations. But what if the sin becomes increasingly prominent, destructive of spiritual life and the ministry of the parishioner? What if the person persists and compounds his or her sin? What ought to be the pastoral response? What will the law say if the minister tells? What about the pastor's duty to the church versus his spiritual duty to the unrepentant counselee?

CLERGY CONFIDENTIALITY

The kind of confidentiality claimed in these church discipline cases should not be confused with a related but somewhat different legal right often referred to as "clergy confidentiality." This refers to the right of a clergyman to remain silent and refuse to testify in court as to communications with a "penitent." In law this is often called the "clergy-penitent privilege."[1]

We have already noted the concept of a "privilege" that creates some exception from a duty or requirement. The clergy-penitent privilege is the right of persons who have communicated certain confidential information to the clergy in the context of pastoral ministry to prevent testimony in court regarding such communications. Such testimony is thus said to be "inadmissible."[2] In some states the privilege is also held by the clergy who may refuse to testify even with a penitent's permission regarding such matters.[3]

Like most privileges it exists not because there is some doubt about the relevance of the testimony or its reliability but because of a social policy of encouraging rather than discouraging persons from confession or seeking pastoral counsel. The Minnesota Supreme Court noted the reasons:

The fundamental thought is that one may safely consult his spiritual adviser. . . . The purpose of the statute is one of large public policy . . . based in part on the idea that the human being does sometimes have need of a place of penitence and confession and spiritual discipline. When any person enters that secret chamber, this statute closes the door upon him and civil authority turns away its ear.[4]

Besides the social policy behind the privilege, the fact it is known that many clergymen would refuse to testify in any event may encourage the protection. As Ponder, writing in *Liberty* magazine, noted:

Generally ministers will not testify, regardless of what the trial judge says or does to them. The Catholic priest, for example, would be subject to excommunication for breaking the seal of the confessional. From his viewpoint, the court's penalty is to be preferred to the church's penalty.[5]

The origin of this privilege can be traced to those traditions, primarily Catholic, in which there is a requirement that members confess regularly to their priest and where the priests are under an absolute religious duty not to reveal these secrets.[6]

In England the privilege has not been recognized since the Restoration in 1660,[7] and, thus, was not a part of the common law influencing American law. In the United States, however, the privilege has been more favor-

ably received. In 1813, perhaps the earliest
case, a New York court held largely on free
exercise grounds that a Catholic priest
should not be compelled to reveal what he
had heard under the Sacrament of Penance.
The court declared:

It is essential to the free exercise of religion, that
its ordinances should not be administered—that
ceremonies as well as its essentials should be
protected. . . . Secrecy is the essence of penance.
The sinner will not confess, nor will the priest receive his confession, if the veil of secrecy is
removed.[8]

Interestingly, some early courts declined to
give the same privilege to Protestants since
the secrecy of the confessional did not constitute a central religious tenet. A New York
case applying such a distinction, *People v.
Smith,* led in part to the adoption by the
New York legislature of the first statute dealing with such a privilege.

Today at least forty-six states provide for
the clergy-penitent privilege by statute, en-
compassing ministers, rabbis, and other religious leaders who perform similar roles.

Often the distinctions among statutes and
the specific language lead to interesting
cases raising such questions as, Who is a
clergyman entitled to the privilege? Does it
extend to nonordained persons acting on behalf of the church such as elders and deacons? And what about those groups that
claim all their members are clergy?

STATUTORY CONDITIONS FOR THE PRIVILEGE. Not all
conversations are privileged, and the statutes usually identify the limits. First, statutes typically provide that the person must
be a clergyman or at least one acting in such
a capacity. Usually a reasonable belief on the
part of the penitent that the other person is
a clergyman will suffice.

Second, the privileged communications must be to a clergyman who is acting in his professional capacity. Random conversations with the clergy will not necessarily be protected.

Third, in some instances courts have held that the communication must be "penitential" in nature; that is, it must be a confession. The New York Court of Appeals held that the priest-penitent privilege arises not because statements are made to a clergyman. Rather something more is needed. . . . "It is only confidential communications made to a clergyman in his spiritual capacity that the law endeavors to protect."[9] Generally, however, the tendency has been to broaden the privilege to include other situations besides traditional confession. The significant role of pastors in general counseling, specifically in marriage counseling, has resulted in revision of statutes or court interpretations that have included these non-confessional communications; but not all courts have extended the privilege to these contexts. As to whether it applies in the context of marriage counseling, a California court indicated that marital counseling communications were not privileged,[10] while a New York court held they were.[11] Some state statutes specifically include marriage counseling. For example, Alabama protects communications when one approaches a clergyman "to enlist help or advice in connection with a marital problem."

Fourth, a number of state statutes have a requirement that the communication be pursuant to a "discipline enjoined by the rules of the church." That is, confession must be in response to a religious duty set forth by the doctrine of the church mandating such confession. Such a requirement reflects a more narrow view of the privilege and roots it not in a general policy of protecting spiritual counsel but in the First Amendment protection against government interference in religious duties. A restrictive view of such language might limit the privilege to Catholic clergy. In *Simrin v. Simrin*, for example, the court noted that the communications in the marriage counseling context were not "a discipline enjoined by the church" and that the statute limited the privilege to such communications. In an Arkansas case the privilege was held not to exist without evidence that the church to which the pastor and penitent belonged made confession a duty.[12] On the other hand many courts read such statutory provisions broadly. In one widely cited case, *In re Swenson*, the Minnesota Supreme Court read "discipline enjoined" to broadly mean the practice of confession:

We are of the opinion that the "confession" contemplated by the statute has reference to a penitential acknowledgement to a clergyman of actual or supposed wrongdoing while seeking religious or spiritual advice, aid or comfort, and that it applies to a voluntary "confession" as well as to one made under a mandate of the church. The clergyman's door should always be open; he should hear all who come regardless of their church affiliation.[13]

EXCEPTIONS TO THE PRIVILEGE. Few privileges are absolute, but especially lately, this general protection of confidentiality and privilege is under some challenge. In a 1984 story, *Time* reporter Richard Ostling noted the controversy when the legal principle of confidentiality competes with a strong social policy, such as stemming the rising tide of child abuse.[14] Widespread attention was drawn to the case of a Florida pastor, John Mellish, to whom Earl Sands, accused of sexually molesting a six-year-old-girl, had surrendered. The prosecutor called Mellish to testify regarding conversation he had had with the accused, and Mellish invoked a right of confidentiality. The court rejected the claim, and when Mellish continued to refuse to testify he was sentenced to sixty days for contempt of court.

At least twenty states have now abolished the clergy-penitent privilege in cases of child abuse. By 1974 all fifty states had mandatory reporting laws often noted as "child protection" statutes. The statutes vary: some involve only medical personnel, but the tendency has been to broaden the group of persons under a duty to report suspected child abuse. Some states have statutory clauses including "any other person." In at least twenty states all privileged communication protections are withdrawn except the attorney-client privilege. Mississippi, for example, specifically indicates that the act of reporting is "not a breach of confidence" and thirty-three states provide a criminal penalty for failure to report such crimes.

These policies clearly clash with the privilege, but some rulings protect the privilege even in child abuse cases. In a 1958 decision, *Mullen v. United States*,[15] the United States Court of Appeals reviewed the conviction of a mother for abuse and willful mistreatment of her children. The decision was reversed on other grounds, but two of the three justices also concurred in an opinion that the admission of the testimony of a Lutheran minister regarding what the woman had told him in preparation for receiving communion was erroneously admitted. "Sound policy—reason and experience—concedes to religious liberty a rule of evidence that a clergymen shall not disclose on a trial the secrets of a penitent's confidential confession. . . ." Circuit

Judge Edgerton in a separate concurring opinion went perhaps even further:

I think a communication made in the reasonable confidence that it will not be disclosed, and in such circumstances that disclosure is shocking to the moral sense of the community, should not be disclosed in a judicial proceeding. . . .[16]

Other recent cases have also pressed the issue of the clergy-penitent privilege. In Arizona a Pentecostal pastor, David Crumbaugh, was given a six-month sentence and one thousand dollar fine for refusing to testify about what the wife of a convicted child killer told him while he counseled them both during the murder trial. And in one state, pastors publicly announced they would disobey a new statute requiring them to report suspected child abuse.

As Ostling noted, regardless of what the courts say, most clergymen continue to invoke the privilege and the "question is whether they will be jailed for doing so."

CONFIDENTIALITY AND CHURCH DISCIPLINE

The "privilege" in regard to court "testimony" is not really the same concept as the kind of confidentiality raised by the church discipline cases, nor is it the primary type expected by the counselee. The counselee does not merely expect that the pastor won't testify in a court or call the cops but that he won't "blab" at all.

In the context of church discipline, the critical aspect of confidentiality is whether there is a relationship creating a legitimate and binding expectation of confidentiality so that its breach is a kind of clergy malpractice, a negligence created by the breach of the pastor's duty to keep secrets.[17]

As churches are increasingly involved in ministries of pastoral counseling, there is a tendency to uncritically adopt a secular counseling style including all the assumptions about confidentiality that properly prevail in secular counseling. And certainly the general concept that persons seeking pastoral care are not going to have their shared secrets made public is reasonable.

But we have noted the conflict between the biblical admonitions about pastoral and church care and any notions of absolute secrecy. In Matthew 18 it is clear that if "counseling" fails, the church is to further its discipline even to the point of public rebuke and expulsion. The secret is to be made known, brought to light that it might be made manifest. As Robert Illman noted writing in the *Presbyterian Journal,* "We have too often been guilty of encouraging an expectation of confidentiality that is inconsistent with our biblical responsibilities."[18]

The more a church counseling program, whether separately staffed or simply part of the pastoral ministry of the staff, takes on the style and character of a secular counseling operation, the more reasonable it is for counselees to assume that secrecy is a guarantee. Such an expectation may be directly encouraged by many pastoral counselors.

The question has not only legal dimensions but pastoral ones as well. The pastoral ministry of the church does depend on a sense of trust that secrets are not revealed. It is important for pastors who become possessors of powerful secrets about others to be scrupulous. If word gets out that a pastor can't be trusted, few will confide in him. But there are limits, and those biblical limits are not simply the legal limits of physical harm to other persons.

Unless the church through its teaching and counseling makes clear that while confidentiality is an aspect of the church counseling ministry it is not absolute, church discipline based on facts that emerge from counseling settings will continue to be legally troublesome.

There is no problem with pursuing church discipline when facts are obtained from independent and clearly non-confidential sources. But where the only source is pastoral counseling settings, the courts may well apply a test of asking whether or not the counselee-parishioner had a reasonable belief that the communications would be held in confidence.

Where courts find there was an expectation of confidentiality that has been breached, the counselor may be vulnerable to actions for "negligence" or a breach of a fiduciary duty.[19]

Of course, even where confidentiality is properly presumed, there may be limits as we have already noted in the case of child abuse reporting statutes. Recent cases raise other exceptions where the secret may be revealed in spite of expectations of confidentiality. One exception that may affect church ministries is the situation where the confidence not only may be revealed, but there may be a duty to disclose it.

A DUTY TO WARN?

The protective privilege ends where the public peril begins.[20]

When is information obtained in a situation of expected confidentiality so vital that one not only may but must reveal it? One guideline is whether the revealed information has to do with past acts, or whether it deals in part with future acts. Lawyers, for example, have a privilege not to reveal confidences from their clients regarding past acts, even heinous crimes, but the privilege does not cover contemplated future criminal acts.

Another factor is whether or not there is a real physical danger to third persons. Public policy interests will certainly be greater where there is ongoing danger to other people.

A case that raised both of these dimensions was *Tarasoff v. Regents.* In 1968 a student at the University of California at Berkeley became distraught over his rejection by a girlfriend. He sought professional counseling and in the process of conversations with a psychologist threatened to kill Tanya, the former girlfriend. Later the agitated lover murdered Tanya. Her parents sued the psychologist and others for negligence because they failed to warn Tanya of the threats. The California Supreme Court in reviewing the case held that when a therapist realizes a third person is in danger, there is a duty to warn that person. The Court noted a "duty to exercise reasonable care to protect the foreseeable victim." The Court concluded that "in our risk-infected society we can hardly tolerate the further exposure to danger that would result from a concealed knowledge of the therapist that his patient was lethal."[21]

The duty to warn has been included in some codes of conduct for mental health professionals, but there is no such uniformly accepted guide for clergy. When is there a "right" to reveal, and when might there even be a "duty"?

MINIMIZING PROBLEMS. Given both legal and ethical considerations, how ought churches and pastors to treat "confidential" information? What policies are appropriate or even mandated?

The most critical legal issue today regarding traditional protections of clergy confidentiality in regard to "testimony" is balancing the interests in protecting such communications (for reasons of both public policy and religious liberty) against concerns for protecting third persons (e.g., abused children). This may well create severe tensions for clergy to whom abusive parents come for help. If the clergyman promises help but advises he must first call the police, the number of such persons seeking help will surely diminish. On the other hand, failure to take action may result in tragedies for children.

It may be critical for pastors to distinguish between situations where the acts for which one seeks help are in the past and where the conduct is likely to continue. Where one comes to confess past acts that are highly unlikely to continue, it is understandable that many clergy will not report such instances for reasons of spiritual duty or prudence. Where there is a continuing risk of harm to others, some action would seem to be legally and morally required, though there may be alternatives to notifying state authorities. When parents seek help they may consent to various reasonable and adequate interim remedies, such as placing the threatened children with relatives while the parents commit themselves to intensive counseling. Of course, clergy who take such steps may be liable under the law not only for failure to report, but should their remedies turn out to be inadequate to protect the children, they may well bear enormous legal liability and moral responsibility.

In regard to church discipline and counseling areas where there is a reasonable expectation of confidentiality, courts may well hold clergy liable if they reveal confidences to others such as church elders or boards. Unless the commonly held expectation of privacy and confidentiality is somehow negated, the pastor may be obliged not to reveal such information.

While this expectation of confidentiality may be overcome by specific statements (disclaimers) and by clearly established principles taught in the church, these may prove inadequate. Much pastoral counseling is simply not done formally but in the process of normal conversation where one does not begin with disclaimers, and in any event the use of such may well serve to shut off counseling. The clarity of disclaiming confidentiality may require it to be so prominent that it would create an erroneous impression of no confidentiality when in fact the church might want to indicate only that there are limits imposed by biblical principles and that communications would be held as confidential as possible within these limits.

If the only source of information is one where there is a reasonable expectation of confidentiality, clergy and counselor may be obliged to respect that confidence. In such a situation, it may be appropriate not to reveal the information even if it seems relevant to the church's ministry and church discipline. That does not bar efforts to encourage the counselees to "own up" to their conduct, to advise them to remove themselves from positions of leadership inconsistent with their continuing conduct, to suggest to appropriate committees that certain persons might not be best to serve in given positions, or in certain circumstances to remove persons from leadership positions. And, as noted, one may proceed with church discipline if the information has come to the attention of the church through other, nonconfidential means. As in *Guinn,* where there is no secret about what is going on, there is no confidence to respect at least as to the basic facts.

On the other hand if information has been obtained in confidence, and whether or not there is potential legal liability, the pastor or church leaders may choose to disclose limited information both in terms of the scope of the audience and the extent of information revealed. "Tell it to the church" is not a license for gossip or a refuge for moral Peeping Toms. There are good reasons for respecting confidences, and even church discipline does not require that the guilty be paraded before the church.

What is important for purposes of church discipline is to carefully assess (1) the church's counseling practices, (2) the likely expectations of parishioners and counselees, (3) whether the church wishes to overcome any expectations it believes are inconsistent with its doctrines, (4) in specific instances, whether or not there is a potential breach of confidence if information is provided others, and (5) whether or not possible disclosure requires a change in the manner in which the church will proceed.

The issue of confidentiality is a mine field not only of legal claims but of troublesome church policy and potentially surprised penitents.

NOTES

[1]For more extensive resources on clergy confidentiality, see William Tiemann and John Bush, *The Right to Silence* (Nashville: Abingdon Press, 1983); Yellin, "The Clergy-Penitent Privilege," 23 *Santa Clara L. Rev.* 95 (1983); Annotation: "Matters to Which the Privilege Covering Communication to Clergymen and Spiritual Advisers Extends," 71 A.L.R.3d 794 (1976); Annotation: "Who Is 'Clergyman' or the Like Entitled to Assert the Privilege Attaching to Communications to Clergymen or Spiritual Advisors," 49 A.L.R.3d 1205 (1973).

[2]The clergy-penitent privilege is a "rule of evidence"; that is, a rule relating to what kind of evidence or testimony is admissible in a civil or criminal proceeding.

[3]The legal issue is, Who holds the privilege? In general the view is that the penitent holds the privilege and may waive the right to claim it. Normally, however, the clergy may assert it on behalf of a penitent absent any indication the penitent has deliberately chosen to waive the privilege. In some states the language would seem to indicate that the clergy also have a privilege independent of that of the penitent, e.g., California Evid. Code. §1034 (West): "A clergyman, whether or not a party, has a privilege to refuse to disclose a penitential communication if he claims the privilege."

[4]*In re Swenson,* 237 N.W. 589, 591 (1931), citing in part *Reutkemeier v. Nolte,* 179 Iowa 342, 161 N.W. 290, 293 (1917).

[5]Ponder, "Will Your Pastor Tell?" *Liberty,* May-June 1978, 3. Church policy itself varies. The Lutheran Church bylaws provide an exception to confidentiality "in order to prevent the commission of a crime." The Catholic church, however, provides no exception, noting that "no cause, however great, whatever the circumstances, will justify its violation. The seal is inviolable. . . ." See the *New Catholic Encyclopedia,* cited by Yellin, 147.

[6]See twenty-first canon of the Lateran Council, 1215.

[7]There is some debate about whether English courts formally recognized the privilege in law in the pre-Reformation period. Certainly it was not absolute. In *Garnets Case* in 1606, Father Garnet had been the spiritual adviser to Guy Fawkes and others allegedly involved in the attempt to assassinate James I. The plot failed, and Garnet was called to testify on any conversations with the defendants. He refused and was tried and found guilty of "having knowledge of a treasonous plot." He is now considered a martyr of the "seal of the confession."

If there was a legal privilege before the Reformation, it was clearly not a part of English law after the Reformation and the Restoration in 1660. While confession remained a central part of the life of the Anglican community, it was no longer compulsory. (Canon 113, Anglican Canons of 1603.) The Sacrament of Confession is held inviolable, but an exception is made where one's knowledge of a crime would subject him to capital punishment if he did not reveal it. Blackstone makes no mention of it in his famous *Commentaries,* and a long line of English cases deny the privilege. In *Normanshaw*

v. Normanshaw, an action for divorce, the Vicar had refused to disclose the substance of an admission made to him. The court declared that "it was not to be supposed for a single moment that a clergyman had any right to withhold information from a court of law." Cited by 8 J. Wigmore, Wigmore on Evidence, § 2394 at 869, 70 n.4 (McNaughten rev. 1961).

[8]See a report of this case in "Privileged Communications to Clergyman," Catholic Lawyer (1955), 207.

[9]Keenan v. Gigante, 47 N.Y.2d 160, 167, 390 N.E.2d 1151, 1154, 417 N.Y.S.2d 226, 229 (1979).

[10]Simrin v. Simrin, 233 Cal. App. 2d 90, 43 Cal. Rptr. 376 (1965).

[11]Kruglikov v. Kruglikov, 29 Misc. 2d 17, 217 N.Y.S.2d 845 (1961), appeal dismissed, 16 A.D.2d 735, 226 N.Y.S. 931 (1962).

[12]Sherman v. State, 170 Ark. 148, 279 S.W. 353 (1926).

[13]In re Swenson, 183 Minn. 602, 604-05, 237 N.W. 589, 591 (1931).

[14]Richard Ostling, "Confidence and the Clergy," Time, 1 Oct. 1984, 66.

[15]Mullen v. United States, 263 F.2d 275 (D.C. Cir. 1958).

[16]263 F.2d at 281 (Edgerton, J., concurring).

[17]This alleged type of clergy malpractice should be distinguished from the type alleged in the well-publicized California case Nally v. Grace Community Church of the Valley, No. NCC 18668-B (L.A. County Super. Ct., filed Mar. 31, 1980). A suit was brought by the parents of Ken Nally alleging that the Grace Community Church and its pastor, John MacArthur, were negligent in failing to refer a suicidal counselee to "professionals," and in training, selecting, and hiring "lay counselors." Of course, in such cases, establishing the nature of the "duty" is extremely difficult because there are no accepted standards of spiritual counseling, and many commentators have expressed concern that the courts not impose a secular model of counseling on the church. See Ericsson, "Clergy Malpractice: Ramifications of a New Theory," 16 Val. U.L. Rev. 163 (Fall 1981).

[18]Robert S. Illman, "Confidentiality and the Law: The Church's Right to Discipline," Presbyterian Journal, 26 Dec. 1984, 9.

[19]In all negligence claims, the basic nature of the legal action is the allegation that there was a duty (here it is a duty of confidentiality), a breach of that duty (the dis-

closure) that has been the cause of damage (pecuniary or other).

[20]*Tarasoff v. Regents,* 17 Cal. 3d 425, 442, 551 P.2d 334, 349, 131 Cal. Rptr. 14, 27 (1976).

[21]*Tarasoff v. Regents,* 551 P.2d at 347, 348 (1976). In another California case a court rejected a claim that a psychiatrist had a duty to reveal to parents disclosures of their daughter about conditions that might lead her to commit suicide, holding that that duty arose only in regard to risks of assault on third persons, not where the danger is self-inflicted. *Bellah v. Greeson,* 81 Cal. App. 3d 614; 146 Cal. Rep. 535 (1978).

7

. . . AND NOTHING BUT THE TRUTH

"It seems to me that you have played a con game with Mrs. Youngblood and that is what I call you, is a con man; you have crooked ways." Those were the tough words of board member C. G. Weeks to Rev. W. D. Joiner when on December 10, 1976, the thirteen members of the Louisiana District Board of the United Pentecostal Church met to hear the allegations of misconduct brought by Rev. Ora Cripps Youngblood against one of its ministers, Rev. W. D. Joiner, concerning his business transactions with her. The board, after hearing the complaints, unanimously passed a resolution noting that the conduct of Joiner was "not right legally, morally, or as a Christian and certainly not as a minister." They had called on him to apologize for his actions, but given his failure to do so and his disrespect for the board they recommended that Rev. Joiner "be dropped from the ministerial fellowship of the United Pentecostal Church."

Rev. Joiner's response was to sue the thirteen members of the board for their action, alleging defamation; he also sued five members of the board, including Weeks, for statements made at the meeting.[1]

The case illustrates the potential for lawsuits against churches and church leaders in civil contexts based not on the invalidity of their dismissal or challenging the power of the church to dismiss its members, but rather alleging that in so doing the church and its leaders have *defamed* the disciplined person. In spite of the reluctance of the courts to entertain any challenge to the right of a church or association to dismiss members, the courts will consider a case for money damages based on defamation.

Indeed, historically the most common tort action out of church discipline contexts has been for defamation, either libel or slander. Libel is defamation in written form (sometimes including radio and TV) and slander is spoken.

DEFAMATION DEFINED

Black's famous law dictionary defines defamation as "The offense of injuring a person's character, fame or reputation by false and malicious statements."[2] The prestigious American Law Institute defines it as follows:

A communication which tends so to harm the reputation of another as to lower him in the estimation of the community or to deter third persons from associating or dealing with him.[3]

It is unnecessary here to trace all the complexities and nuances of defamation law.[4] The basic concept is that one's reputation has been "injured." To establish a case for defamation, the "elements" (aspects of the facts) that must be proven by the plaintiff are (1) the use of defamatory words (language that injures the person in his reputation), (2) the communication was "of or concerning" the plaintiff,[5] (3) its "publication" to a third person,[6] (4) a showing of resulting damage to the reputation of the plaintiff,[7] and (5) in some cases "fault" such as negligence or malice on the part of the defendant.[8]

In general, any statement is defamatory that would damage the reputation of someone in the community in general or of any substantial and respectable group. Some allegations are clearly defamatory, while others might depend on the circumstances. In certain circumstances, courts have held it defamatory to say that a person attempted suicide or that he is immoral or unchaste, is a hypocrite, a drunkard, a liar, even a "rotten egg." One court held that the statement that one had been expelled from a church was defamatory.[9]

Certainly many of the "charges" against persons in church discipline cases are damaging to their reputations. Consequently, disciplined persons have frequently alleged that oral or written statements made about them during the course of church discipline procedures constituted defamation.

While it is not common, plaintiffs have been successful in defamation complaints that have arisen out of church discipline contexts. It is important to recognize that what the plaintiff wins when he is successful in such a case is not reinstatement of membership. In defamation cases the validity of the expulsion or suspension is not at issue. The plaintiff, if successful, will win a money judgment (damages) against the defendants who were directly involved in the defamatory communications, such as the persons who initiated the false charges or who falsely testified.[10]

FOR THE DEFENSE

When a lawsuit makes allegations of defamation there are two basic lines of defense. First, one may seek to convince the judge or jury that the plaintiff has not proven all the "elements" of the case. For instance, there is no proof of "damage" to the reputation (e.g., it was already damaged), or there is no "publication."[11]

Second, and more commonly, one may raise one of several "affirmative defenses" to such actions. In the context of church discipline cases, the two most important are the defenses of *truth* and of *qualified privilege*.

DEFENSE NUMBER ONE: TRUTH. Truth is an absolute defense against an allegation of defamation, no matter how great the damage to the plaintiff's reputation. The defendant is responsible for proving the truthfulness of the statements to the jury or judge,[12] since he is the one who issued the allegedly defamatory statement.[13]

Thus, if the allegations contained in charges against church members subject to discipline are true, those making the allegations are not liable for defamation.[14]

In a number of the lawsuits against the churches cited at the outset of this book, there were no allegations of defamation. That is perhaps because the plaintiffs knew that truth was an absolute defense; if what was said about the plaintiffs in church or on the street corner was true, there is no case in defamation.

The lesson is this: tell the truth, and you will not be liable for defamation.[15]

DEFENSE NUMBER TWO: QUALIFIED PRIVILEGE. It is important to understand the nature of a "privilege" and specifically a "qualified privilege." These concepts are crucial, both to defamation actions and in determining the outcome in other actions such as invasion of privacy (as in the *Guinn* case).

A privilege is an immunity or exemption
from a duty that would otherwise bind a person. It is "a right, power, franchise, or immunity held by a person or class, against or
beyond the course of the law."[16]

Common examples are the constitutional
"privilege" against self-incriminating testimony,[17] or the "priest-penitent privilege"
that exempts clergy from testifying about
statements made to them in the course of
their pastoral duties. In the law of defamation, a privilege would be "an exemption
from liability for the speaking or publishing
of defamatory words."

Such privileges may be either absolute or
qualified (conditional). Absolute privileges,
as the name suggests, are total; they are un-
conditional. In a defamation case, if the defamer holds absolute privilege, he is not
liable regardless of his motive or purposes.
Such privileges are rare; they apply to statements made in judicial proceedings, to statements by legislators in their official
capacities, and historically to statements
made between spouses. As these examples
illustrate, the reason behind these absolute
privileges is a public policy purpose—a basic
concern that in those situations the courts
do not want persons to be subjected to defamation suits.

A qualified or conditional privilege, however, is not total. It may be lost under some circumstances. In the law of defamation, the
privilege assumes "good faith," and if the
defamer is shown to have made the defamatory statement with malice or with knowledge of its falsity, the privilege would be
lost. But if the qualified privilege is found to
exist there is no liability for libel or slander.
Even where every element of the plaintiff's
case has been proved and truth is no de-

fense because the statements were, as it turned out, false, still, if a privilege applies there is no liability! Therefore, even if truth is not available as an absolute defense, a qualified privilege may preclude liability.

Obviously, the qualified privilege is an important principle and one that can protect persons who otherwise might be liable. Why would the law provide such an exemption? In the *Joiner* case discussed at the beginning of the chapter the court said such a privilege

arises from the social necessity of permitting full and unrestricted communication concerning a matter in which the parties have an interest or duty, without inhibiting free communication in such instances by the fear that the communicating party will be held liable in damages if the good faith communications turns out to be inaccurate.[18]

Who has a qualified privilege? One frequently cited discussion of the scope of a qualified privilege in defamation explains what kinds of communications are protected by this privilege:

communications made in good faith upon any subject matter in which the party communicating has an interest or in reference to which he has a duty to a person having a corresponding duty or interest, although the duty be not a legal one, but of a moral or social character . . . and it arises from the necessity of full and unrestricted communication concerning a matter in which the parties have an interest of duty.[19]

This definition embodies these critical elements: (1) the statements must be made in good faith; (2) there must be a legitimate interest or duty on the part of the communicator (the "duty" may be either legal or moral in nature); and (3) the communication must be to one with a similar interest or duty.

Common situations where this qualified

privilege is found are in communications between an employer and employee related to job responsibilities or among members of fraternal associations or labor organizations.[20] What about churches?

It is not surprising under these principles that courts have generally recognized that a qualified privilege exists for certain statements made in good faith, even if defamatory and false, in the context of church discipline proceedings. In fact, the Restatement (Second) of Torts, Section 596, discusses common interests as they apply to religious groups:

The common interest of members of religious, charitable or other nonprofit associations . . . is recognized as sufficient to support a privilege for communication among themselves concerning the qualifications of the officers and members and their participation in the activities of the society. This is true whether the defamatory matter relates to alleged misconduct of some other member that makes him undesirable for continued membership or the conduct of a prospective member. . . .[21]

A modern California case illustrates both the scope of the privilege and the limits. Rev. A. L. Brewer and E. W. Fisher brought an action for libel against the Second Baptist Church of Los Angeles and several individual defendants (the pastor, chairman, and secretary of the deacons). Previously Brewer and others had unsuccessfully sued the church to have an election set aside. The deacons and the pastor, upset with this, then voted to expel Brewer and his co-plaintiff from the church for their involvement in the lawsuit against the church. Two of the defendants drew up charges. The statement of charges noted the "vile spirit and utter disrespect for leadership" on the part of Brewer, that they "hurt the prestige and good name of the church" and concluded

We finally charge that both of these men have by their unwarranted actions and downright falsehood revealed themselves as totally unworthy of the continued confidence, respect and fellowship of a great church which they have so grievously wronged.

Brewer and Fisher were advised of the dismissal proceedings, and the church then voted to "withdraw the hand of fellowship."

Apparently to broadcast its message, the church issued a press release to the local press reporting the action and provided the article on their actions for a newspaper, *The National Baptist Voice*. The article stated that the charges to set aside the election Brewer had initially brought against the church in the dismissed lawsuit had been found to be "false" by the judge.[22]

Brewer and others then sued for defamation. The court had no problem finding the language was defamatory. In fact, the court noted the "charges were designed to injure the plaintiffs' reputations in the church and to cause them to be shunned and avoided." The court noted that "the language was aptly chosen for this purpose."

The court then considered the claim of the church that it had a qualified privilege. The California Civil Code provided for such a privilege in language similar to that cited above.[23] In applying the California rule, the court observed:

Ordinarily, the common interest of the members of a church in church matters is sufficient to give rise to a qualified privilege to communications between members on subjects relating to the church's interest. . . . A privilege would exist if the publication had been made without malice and the occasion had not been abused.

The court proceeded to note, however, that this privilege could be lost in several ways: "(1) by the publisher's lack of belief, or of reasonable grounds for belief, in the truth of the defamatory material, (2) by excessive publication, (3) by . . . an improper purpose, or (4) if the defendant goes beyond the group interest."[24]

The court in reviewing the history of disputes in the congregation found "ample evidence in the record" to support the inference of ill will and malice by Pastor Henderson. The qualified privilege therefore had been lost, and the defendants were liable. The qualified privilege did not give the defendants a "license to overdraw, exaggerate, or to color the facts."

What is good faith? The *Brewer* case illustrates the general statements of law about qualified privileges and the requirement of "good faith." The privilege is lost if the defamer has malice, an admittedly difficult concept to define. The *Brewer* court spoke of a motivation by any cause other than the desire to carry out church discipline in good faith. Other courts have spoken of malice as the use of expulsion proceedings as a "pretense of pretext."

This is, of course, a state of mind and difficult to test directly, but the courts may look to several factors as indicators of a lack of good faith. Certainly the parties must have, in regard to their statements, a "reasonable belief in their truth."[25] Courts have also spoken of ill will and an intention to injure the plaintiff in his profession or an intention to injure the plaintiff's feelings and reputation. Courts have also taken note of such factors as the general tenor of the charges, coloring or exaggerating the facts, failure to state facts fully, vilification or extravagant language, or a complete lack of knowledge of facts in a signed statement.

In *Joiner v. Weeks,* the issue arose of whether or not a qualified privilege existed or whether it had been lost by a lack of good faith. The court found that the meetings and proceedings of the church officials were done in good faith and without malice, noting that meetings were limited to the proper members of the board, and that resolutions and discussions were not circulated to anyone without a legitimate interest.[26]

What constitutes a community of interest? "It is hard to imagine a more obvious example of common interest than that which is shared by the members of a church,"[27] observed a New Hampshire court.

Besides good faith, the other basic requirement for qualified privilege is that the communication take place between persons who have a legitimate common interest or duty to share such information. And the nearly universal decision of courts has been to find such a legitimate common interest within the church in carrying out its affairs, including the discipline of its members.

But how broad is this community? Is it the whole church or only the leaders? What about sharing information with sister churches as in the Collinsville case? or publishing it in a newsletter? When does the legitimate right of the community to have access to information, even if it turns out to be wrong, become abused and an occasion for destructive gossip?

Such questions raise not only legal issues but theological ones as well. Clearly, a Christian theology will see the church as a community. As the Bible makes it clear, it is a body whose parts are concerned with each other. It is a community of confession, of mutual accountability, of common and reciprocal admonition. Its members have a clear moral duty toward one another, and the church is theologically thought to create by its very nature a community of interest. The church will have a clear perception of the sort of information in regard to which there is a legitimate common interest, such as the moral health of the community of faith, the purity of doctrine, and the practice of its adherents.

Of course, church traditions may vary the roles given different persons within the body and the duties of pastoral oversight or church discipline that fall to various members. These differences in church governance may confuse the courts unfamiliar with church structures and their theological underpinnings. It is no wonder that courts may at times find it difficult to draw hard and fast lines.

If, as we have suggested earlier, there is a growing clash between the church's own self-understanding of its nature and scope of responsibility and the surrounding culture's perception of what the church is about, then courts may render surprising decisions as they seek to apply concepts of "legitimate" interest and "duty."

What kinds of disclosures and persons are covered by the scope of community interest? While the case law is generally quite old and must always be read in light of the specific facts of each case, the pattern seems to be to extend the privilege, once it is established, to a fairly broad range of situations. One old case frequently cited suggested that the privilege protects persons bringing charges, testifying, voting, or announcing a result as long as it is done in good faith and within the authority of the church.[28] Other cases have held that the privilege covers the words of a presiding officer within his line of duty if he uttered them believing in their truth and from a sense of duty,[29] words of members of a church tribunal investigating charges,[30] the publication of charges in a denominational journal privileged due to common interest and privilege not lost by incidentally coming to the attention of nonmembers,[31] and recommendations by investigatory panels.[32] The privilege has been extended to include a pastor reading the sentence of expulsion to the congregation,[33] a charge made by a church member with honest intention of examining fitness for membership,[34] and letters by church members to church officials having authority to act, such as to a bishop concerning a priest or to church deacons regarding the pastor or his wife.[35]

These decisions seem to rest on the relationship of the communications to the regular or official systems and bodies within the church that have duties in regard to investigation or discipline. In these cases, the "duty" is more obvious, resting not simply on common interest but on identified responsibilities and structures. A few decisions have applied the privilege when it is outside the normal, official disciplinary structures or procedures of the church, such as when church members discuss among themselves charges against members or a pastor.

But what if the "publication" goes beyond the church itself? There certainly are some limits, even if they are unclear. In one case it was held that slanderous words about one clergyman to another clergyman of the same denomination and to a church at which the slandered clergyman was preaching were not privileged even though the purpose was in the context of a controversy about whether the church ought to employ the clergyman.[36] Likewise a letter by one minister to a minister and to the ministerial association

stating that another minister was unfit for
the ministry, was held not privileged because the minister owed no duty to the association and had no interest in the removal of
the minister.[37]

And watch out if you criticize the evangelist. In *Haynes v. Robertson* it was held that a
member's slanderous statement about an
evangelist who preached in the church but
who was not then a member nor a pastor of
the church was not privileged since the
church had no valid reason to evaluate the
evangelist at that time.[38] And in *Ballew v.
Thompson* when members of the same
church were discussing another church
member, it was held that no qualified privilege existed where there was no evidence of
a duty upon members to give information
about each other's characters.[39]

We believe courts have properly held that
not all publication outside the church itself
necessarily destroys the privilege. In *Redgate
v. Rousch* the elders of a Church of Christ in
Wilmington, Kansas, found their pastor unworthy of his office. They published a notice
in church papers distributed over a number
of midwestern states, noting the unfitness of
their preacher, charging him with "insubordination," and indicating they did not consider
him "worthy of the confidence of the
brotherhood."

The Kansas Supreme Court held that "if
the statements were published in good faith,
and in what was honestly deemed to be an
official or moral duty toward other church
members, and for the benefit and protection
of the church organization at large ... it is
privileged and protected." The Kansas Court
concluded, "If the plaintiff was unworthy of
his high calling, the defendants, interested
in the welfare of the denomination throughout the land, would appear to have been jus-

tified in warning other members and congregations." The fact that others might have inadvertently seen the publication did not destroy the privilege.[40]

Similarly, the reading of the charges to the whole congregation, even when non-members were present, was held not to have been so broad as to destroy the privilege.[41]

CONCLUSION

It is clear that churches and their leaders may be held liable in defamation for accusations that damage the reputation of church members who are under investigation or discipline. This liability, however, may be avoided in two ways. First, the church must scrupulously adhere to truth in both fact and implication. The potential for defamation liability is thus eliminated.

Secondly, further protection may be added by assuring that the communication of charges takes place within the parameters of the church's clear common interest and sense of moral duty. This latter protection of the qualified privilege is more elusive since it requires the court to interpret what is a legitimate interest and duty. But churches may assist that interpretation by the clear enunciation of their understanding of the church and the responsibilities of members and leaders.

NOTES

[1]*Joiner v. Weeks, et al.*, 383 So. 2d 101 (La. App. 1976).

[2]*Black's Law Dictionary*, rev. 4th ed. (St. Paul: West Publishing, 1968), 505.

[3]Restatement (Second) of Torts § 559 (1976).

[4]It is not an easy area of law to master and one that is constantly shifting. One scholar noted, "No branch of litigation has been more fertile than this (whether plain-

tiffs be moved by a keen sense of honour, or by the delight of carrying on personal controversies under the protection and with the solemnities of civil justice). . . ." Sir Frederick Pollack, *Law of Torts,* 13th ed. (London: Stevens & Sons, Limited, 1929), 243.

[5]Usually there will be no doubt as to whom the communication refers, but if there is uncertainty, it may be shown by the circumstances.

[6]Publication here obviously does not mean publication in the sense of "publishing" a book. It includes any communication to a third person. There must be someone else who is aware of the defamatory statements.

[7]Certain types of libel referred to as "libel per se" do not traditionally require a showing of damages. These are statements that have been felt by courts to so clearly damaging that no further proof is necessary. Allegations of immorality and allegations of unfitness for a profession are included in this category. Thus many statements made in a church disciplinary context would fall into the "libel per se" category.

[8]Increasingly, in order to minimize inhibiting free political discourse and freedom of the press, courts are requiring a showing of some fault in defamation cases. In cases brought by public figures (prominent political figures, for example) against media defendants (TV, newspapers, magazines, etc.), the Supreme Court now requires a showing of "actual malice"—publication in spite of knowledge of its falsity or reckless disregard for its truth or falsity. Thus a public figure such as Ariel Sharon faced difficulty in winning a judgment against *Time* magazine.

[9]*Servatius v. Pichel,* 34 Wis. 292 (1874).

[10]See *Swafford v. Keaton,* 29 Ga. App. 13, 113 S.E. 67 (1922); *Whittaker v. Carter,* 26 N.C. 461 (1844); *Dial v. Holter,* 6 Ohio St. 228 (1856) in which judgments were rendered against church members who brought false charges or were witnesses who falsely testified at expulsion trials or before investigators.

[11]The Appellant's Brief before the Oklahoma Supreme Court for the Collinsville Church of Christ argued that there had been no "publication" of the statements on which invasion of privacy was found. Counsel cited an early Missouri defamation case in which the court held there was no publication when the pastor read resolutions excommunicating a member in church services and also made the resolutions available to church members. The Missouri court held that such communications

did not constitute "publication within the meaning of defamation law." *Landis v. Campbell,* 79 Mo. 433 (1833).

[12]The judge or jury is referred to as the "trier of fact"; that is, the person or persons who decide all factual questions based on the evidence, such as whether or not a person said a certain thing. If there is a jury, then the jury will be the "trier of fact" (the judge always decides the law), but in some civil cases there may be no jury and then the judge will also be the "trier of fact."

[13]The one who has the responsibility is said to have the "burden of proof." While the plaintiff has the "burden of proof" regarding the allegations of his basic case, such as the publication of an injurious statement, because he must "prove" his case, the burden of proof for all "affirmative defenses" such as "truth" is on the one asserting that defense, namely, the defendant.

[14]Of course, the reader can appreciate two things: first, there may be considerable difference of opinion about the "truth" of the allegations that are the basis of the lawsuit; and second, some allegations are not very easily susceptible to "proof." For example, a charge that one is "contentious," "a gossip," or, as in one case, "devilish" cannot be proved with precision. Of course, some technically true statements might in fact communicate an untruth. For example, the statement "Well, at least he doesn't get drunk on Sundays" may be true of an abstainer, but it implies something else.

[15]This assumes, of course, that you can establish the probability of the truth of the communication. In civil trials you do not need to "prove" to the trier of fact that something is certain or "beyond a reasonable doubt." In these cases you are required simply to prove that it is more likely true than false; the weight of the evidence, the "preponderance of the evidence," must tip on your side.

[16]*Black's Law Dictionary,* 1359.

[17]U.S. Constitution. Amend. V.

[18]Citing *Toomer v. Breaux,* 146 So. 2d 723 (La. App. 3d Cir., 1962). Restatement (Second) of Torts § 592 (1977) also speaks of the public policy behind a qualified privilege in order to assure the flow of true information.

[19]*Southern Ice Co. v. Black,* 136 Tenn. 391, 189 S.W. 861, 863 (1916). See 33 Am. Jur. Libel Slander §126 (1941). Oklahoma law would appear to concur. In *Tuohy v. Halsell,* 128 P. 126, 128 (Okla. 1912) the Oklahoma Supreme Court declared that a qualified privilege "extends to all

communications made bona fide upon a subject-matter in which the party communicating has an interest, or in reference to which he has a duty to a person having a corresponding interest or duty, and to cases where the duty is not a legal one, but where it is of a moral or social character or imperfect obligation."

20See Harold A. Jones, "Interest and Duty in Relation to Qualified Privilege," 22 *Mich. L. Rev.*, 441-444 (1924).

21Restatement (Second) of Torts § 596, Commente (1977).

22The suit by the plaintiffs had not been dismissed because the charges were "false," but on other grounds. Thus, truth as a defense was not available in the later defamation case.

23Cal. Civ. Code § 47(3)(West).

24*Brewer v. Second Baptist Church*, 32 Cal. 2d 791, 197 P.2d 713, 717 (1948) (numbers added).

25Ibid., 718.

26Citing *Carter v. Catfish Cabin*, 316 So. 2d 517 (La. App. 1975), citing in turn *Madison v. Bolton*, 234 La. 997, 102 So. 2d 443 (1958).

27*Slocinski v. Radwan*, 144 A 787 (N.H. 1929).

28*Kleizer v. Symmes*, 40 Ind. 562 (1872); *Butterworth v. Todd*, 76 N.J.L. 317, 70 A. 139 (1908); and *Shurtleff v. Stevens*, 51 Vt. 501, 31 Am. Rep. 698 (1879); *Servatius v. Pichel*, 34 Wis. 292 (1874); all citing *Farnsworth v. Storrs*, 5 Cush. 412 (Mass. 1850).

29*Anderson v. Malm*, 198 Ill. App. 58 (1916).

30*Kleizer v. Symmes*, 40 Ind. 562 (1872).

31*Redgate v. Rousch*, 61 Kan. 480, 59 P. 1050 (1900); and *Moyle v. Franz*, 267 App. Div. 423, 46 N.Y.S.2d 667, aff'd, 293 N.Y. 842, 59 N.E.2d 437 (1944) (so long as publication circulation is limited to those interested in the affairs of the organization).

32*Lucas v. Case*, 9 Bush. 297 (Ky. 1872); *Bass v. Matthews*, 69 Wash. 214, 124 P. 384 (1912).

33*Farnsworth v. Storrs*, 5 Cush. 412 (Mass. 1850).

34*Jarvis v. Hatheway*, 3 Johns. 180, 3 Am. Dec. 473 (N.Y. 1808).

35*O'Donaghue v. McGovern*, 23 Wend. 26 (N.Y. 1840); *Lawless v. Ellis*, 281 S.W. 1090 (Tex. Civ. App. 1926).

36*Ritchie v. Widdemer*, 59 N.J.L. 290, 35 825 (1896).

[37]*Shurtleff v. Parker,* 130 Mass. 293, 39 Am. Rep. 454 (1881).

[38]*Haynes v. Robertson,* 190 Mo. App. 156, 175 S.W. 290 (1915).

[39]*Ballew v. Thompson,* 259 S.W. 856 (Mo. App. 1924).

[40]*Redgate v. Rousch,* 61 Kan. 480, 48 L.R.A. 236, 59 P. 1050 (1900). Similarly the publication by an association of ministers of their withdrawal of fellowship from a minister and a requirement that he show cause why he should not be dismissed was held not to lose its privileged character even though it was in denominational papers reaching the general public. *Shurtleff v. Stevens,* 51 Vt. 501, 31 Am. Rep. 698 (1879).

[41]*Landis v. Campbell,* 79 Mo. 433, 49 Am. Rep. 239 (1883).

8

PRIVATE: KEEP OUT!

The poorest man may in his cottage bid defiance to the Crown. It may be frail—its roof may leak—the wind may enter—the rain may enter—but the King of England cannot enter—all his force dares not cross the threshold of the ruined tenement.
William Pitt[1]

For everyone who does evil hates the light, and does not come to the light, lest his deeds should be exposed. But he who does what is true comes to the light, that it may be clearly seen that his deeds have been wrought in God.
John 3:20, 21, RSV

Was Marian Guinn's private world invaded by the busybodies of the Collinsville Church of Christ? Were the elders merely ecclesiastical Peeping Toms who, having pried themselves into her personal life, compounded their wrongs by "telling all" to the church? Should they have observed the "keep out" sign she erected around her affairs? Should they pay—literally—for their meddling? She thought so, or at least her lawyers did!

When Marian Guinn's lawyers filed their suit against the Collinsville Church of Christ, they asserted

that on or about the 27th day of September, 1981, the Defendants . . . give [sic] publicity to certain matters concerning the private life of Plaintiff and did thereby invade her privacy. . . . That said matters were publicized to the congregation, members and attendants of the Church of Christ of Collinsville, Oklahoma. That the publication . . . was highly offensive and was not of legitimate concern to said persons or to the public.[2]

Marian's attorney has not been alone in seeking help in such allegations. James Shive in his suit alleged that

the defendants . . . did give publicity to certain matters concerning the private life of James L. Shive and did thereby invade his privacy [and] that the publication . . . is and was highly offensive and was not of legitimate concern to said persons or to the public . . . and not of public record.[3]

John Kelly's complaint against the church similarly alleged that the defendants "invaded Plaintiff's privacy by intrusion into [his] private affairs, publicly disclosing embarrassing, intimate, and private facts."[4]

Imagine you are counsel for Marian Guinn or other plaintiffs seeking judicial relief from the discipline of the church. On what basis can you "win"? If the church has acted within its own rights of association to establish the conditions of membership, we have seen that it is unlikely the courts will interfere. Actions for defamation will not succeed if the allegations and statements made are true. Even if there are some allegations that prove untrue, the privileges of legitimate interest among the persons acting in good faith would likely defeat any claims. Where then can disgruntled litigants find legal help?

Enter the new torts of "invasion of privacy" and "infliction of emotional distress."

IF AT FIRST YOU DON'T SUCCEED . . .

These torts that allege wrongs to the dignity of the individual are relatively modern and therefore not highly defined. It is unclear precisely what facts will sustain such a claim or what defenses will defeat it. In this area the courts make new laws as often as they interpret them. The scope of these torts, the defenses to them, and the degree to which the Constitution limits such cases as free exercise claims are still largely unknown. Professor McGoldrick has even suggested that the church might have been better off if it had made a clearly false statement about Guinn instead of a true one because the common law and constitutional limits of defamation actions are much clearer than the elusive torts of invasion of privacy and emotional distress. Counsel for plaintiffs turn to these actions hoping they can make the facts fit the newly developing principles of these claims. Perhaps they can "win" here what they could not win under the older types of actions.

SHOULD THE LAW STOP THESE "INVASIONS OF PRIVACY"? What should we think of these legal actions for "invasion of privacy"? Certainly most of us recognize that sometimes people go too far, and the law properly provides a remedy.

In a well-publicized "invasion" case, Jacqueline Onassis counter-sued Galella, an aggressive photographer, alleging that his persistent efforts to photograph her were an invasion of privacy. She sought court orders to protect her and her children.[5] This was the prototype of intrusive surveillance. The court summarized Galella's efforts:

Continuously he has her under surveillance to the point that he is notified of her every movement. He waits outside her residence at all hours. He

follows her about irrespective of what she is doing: trailing her up and down the streets of New
York, chasing her out of the city . . . haunting her
at restaurants (recording what she eats), theaters,
the opera . . . pursuing her when she goes shopping. . . . He studies her habits . . . her shopping
tastes and habits, her preferences for entertainment. . . . He has intruded into her children's
schools, hidden in bushes and behind coat racks
in restaurants, sneaked into beauty salons, bribed
doormen, hatcheck girls, chauffeurs, fishermen in
Greece, hairdressers and schoolboys, and ro-
manced employees. In short, Galella has insinuat-
ed himself into the very fabric of Mrs. Onassis's
life and the challenge to this Court is to fashion
the tool to get him out.

The court, not surprisingly, granted relief
to Mrs. Onassis.

Or consider seeing your picture in some
magazine under circumstances that seem intrusive. While there is generally no liability
for using a picture of a person taken in a
public place, under special circumstances liability exists. For example, in *Daily-Times
Democrat Co. v. Graham,* taking a picture of
a woman in a "fun house" with her dress
blown up was held to be an invasion of privacy.[6] Similarly, in *York v. Story* the circulation in a police station of nude pictures of
the plaintiff was held to be an invasion.[7] A
third example of special circumstances was
the newspaper publication of the X rays of a
woman's pelvic region.[8]

A forbidden intrusion was found in a New
Hampshire case. A married couple sued their
landlord for installing a "listening and recording device" in their bedroom "capable of
transmitting and recording any sounds and
voices originating in said bedroom." Chief
Judge Kenison of the New Hampshire Court
noted that this kind of "intrusion" was offensive to any person and that in intrusion

cases publication or communication to others is not necessary. He concluded:

If the peeping Tom, the big ear and the electronic eavesdropper . . . have a place in the hierarchy of social values, it ought not to be at the expense of a married couple minding their own business in the seclusion of their bedroom.[9]

In cases like these most of us have little trouble with court-imposed limits or civil lawsuits to stop such intrusions. We all need a little "space." Life today is so intense, so overloaded with information! We are constantly observed, polled, questioned, surveyed, numbered. Everyone has our social security number, credit histories, phone number, and addresses. We often feel exposed. Privacy may be an "imaginary luxury" in the modern world.[10]

We have been well-warned by Huxley's *Brave New World* and Orwell's *1984* of the dangers of the ever-present monitor, Big Brother—the secular, omniscient intruder whose prying disintegrates the integrity of individual life in a totalitarian state.

Certain elements of privacy are essential both to freedom and to individuality. "The free man is the private man, the man who still keeps some of his thoughts and judgments entirely to himself, who feels no overriding compulsion to share everything of value with others, not even those he loves and trusts," historian Clinton Rossiter observed.[11]

In a psychological sense, privacy is also prized and essential. We all value our individuality and privacy, our own zones of autonomy that can shelter our "ultimate secrets." In fact, Alan Westin suggests that "the most serious threat to the individual's autonomy is the possibility that someone may penetrate the inner zone and learn his

ultimate secrets . . . penetrat[ing] the individual's protective shell, his psychological ar-
mour, [which] would leave him naked to
ridicule and shame and put him under the
control of those who knew his secrets."[12]
"The individual's sense that it is he who decides when to go 'public' is a crucial aspect
of his feeling of autonomy."[13] Leontine Young
has gone so far as to declare that "without
privacy there is no individuality."[14]

Some, of course, are not seeking privacy so
much as escape. They avoid responsibility,
accountability, even perhaps life itself. It
may be very destructive. Noted psychiatrist
Karen Horney describes persons who seek
an unnatural degree of privacy as one of the
three major types of neurotics in our society:

[This type of neurotic] is like a person in a hotel
room who rarely removes the "Do-Not-Disturb"
sign from his door. . . . He tends to shroud himself
in a veil of secrecy. A patient once told me that at
the age of forty-five he still resented the idea of
God's omniscience quite as much as when his
mother told him that God could look through the
shutters and see him biting his fingernails.[15]

PRIVACY AND THE LAW

Our concern here, however, is not chiefly
with the healthiness or political implications
of certain quests for privacy[16] but with the
development of the legal protections of privacy, especially in the modern tort of "invasion
of privacy."

The law has recently given increasing attention to issues of privacy in the face of
growing threats of electronic intrusions (e.g.,
bugging and wiretaps) and potential abuses
of the massive data banks of information on
each of us—our medical records, credit histories, financial status. Federal and state
laws have sought to protect such information and personal records. Most notable in

this connection is the Federal Privacy Act of 1974. These protections limit *government* disclosure of confidential information. Other statutes prohibit electronic wiretapping by private parties. The protections in law that stop blabbermouths, snoops, and busybodies are not criminal statutes but provisions for civil remedies through lawsuits that may be brought by private persons alleging that they have been wronged, damaged by another's intrusive act; thus the tort of "invasion of privacy."

THE LEGAL CONCEPT OF INVASION OF PRIVACY

Aspects of the legal protection of privacy have existed in Western law and in our constitutional system from its inception. The First Amendment's guarantees directly impact on privacy. Justice Joseph Story in his classic *Commentaries on the Constitution of the United States* noted that these protections were intended to secure the rights of "private sentiment" and "private judgment."[17] The Third Amendment protects our homes against the quartering of troops without permission, the object of which, Story insisted, was "to secure the perfect enjoyment of that great right of the common law, that a man's house shall be his own castle, privileged against all civil and military intrusion."[18] And the Fourth Amendment guarantee against unreasonable searches and seizures is a fundamental building block for defending privacy against government intrusion. Thomas Cooley in his influential treatise on the Constitution written in 1868 spoke of these protections as providing an "immunity in his home against the prying eyes of the government." These provisions of the Bill of Rights are all limits on governmental intrusions.

In addition to limits on the government's reach, there were early legal protections against individual invasions of privacy. For example, common law in early America protected against eavesdropping. In 1831 a Pennsylvania judge upheld a charge against a man who watched a married woman through the window in her home and spread tales about her, commenting:

I consider this as a serious kind of offense. Every man's house is his castle, where no man has a right to intrude for any purpose whatever. No man has a right to pry into your secrecy in your own house. There are very few families where even the truth would not be very unpleasant to be told all over the country. . . . It is important to all persons that our families should be sacred from the intrusion of every person.[19]

But these legal principles protected privacy only indirectly. There was no such thing as a "right to privacy," and one could not sue for its violation. The modern concept of invasion of privacy owes its life to an 1890 *Harvard Law Review* article, "The Right of Privacy," by Samuel D. Warren and Louis D. Brandeis. The article apparently had been stimulated by a Boston newspaper's report of Warren's wife's social activities to which he took great exception. The article argued that there was a "right of privacy" that the law ought to recognize, a right "not arising from contract" or notions merely of private property, but rights "as against the world."[20] They declared:

Of the desirability—indeed of the necessity—of some such protection, there can, it is believed, be no doubt. The press is overstepping in every direction the obvious bounds of propriety and of decency. Gossip is no longer the resource of the idle and of the vicious, but has become a trade . . . column upon column is filled with idle gossip. . . .

Each crop of unseemly gossip, thus harvested, becomes the seed of more, and, in direct proportion to its circulation, results in a lowering of social standards and of morality. . . .

It has been said that this article is the "monument in whose shadow courts deliberate upon claims alleging transgressions of privacy."[21]

The article did not institute a complete and immediate revolution. In the first case after publication that tested the concept of "rights to privacy," a New York court was faced with a suit by a girl whose picture had been used in advertising without her permission.[22] She alleged that her privacy had been invaded. The defendants claimed there was no such thing as a right of privacy. The trial court rendered a judgment for the girl, but the highest court in New York reversed 4-3. Chief Judge Parker declared simply, "There is no precedent for such an action. . . ." The judge worried that if such a principle were permitted

the attempts to logically apply the principle will necessarily result not only in a vast amount of litigation but in litigation bordering on the absurd, for the right of privacy, once established, cannot be confined to the restraint of the publication of a likeness.

The Court suggested that if any such a right were to be asserted, it should come not from the courts but from the legislature.[23] The New York legislature responded in 1903 by enacting the first law protecting privacy: It prohibited the use of any name, portrait, or picture of a living person for purposes of advertising or trade without prior consent. The case illustrates the tendency of the early privacy cases to focus on the unconsented use of a person's name or likeness, usually in a commercial advertising context.

As Judge Parker worried, however, privacy as a right could not be confined to merely legal "restraint of the publication of a likeness." Gradually, a diverse set of acts have all received the generic label "invasions of privacy." Privacy crosses criminal, constitutional, and civil law lines. As we have noted, there are some specific areas where criminal statutes apply, most notably in such areas as "bugging." A major area of constitutional law is developing around this concept of privacy, which focuses on delineating the fundamental rights to privacy against government actions. Our concerns here are chiefly with those aspects of privacy in the civil law—the tort of "invasion of privacy."[24]

Today the law in almost every state recognizes the right of privacy and provides a legal civil remedy for its invasion. Legal scholars and most courts, following an analysis by a prominent torts scholar, William Prosser,[25] have identified four types of invasions of privacy that have been given a legal remedy:

1. *An unauthorized appropriation of a person's name or likeness for commercial advantage* (e.g., using Martina Navratilova's name or picture in connection with Wheaties advertising).

2. *Acts of intrusion into the privacy of one's affairs or seclusion in a way that would be objectionable to a reasonable person*—a kind of prying (e.g., putting a microphone in someone's bedroom).

3. *Putting a person into a false light*—publication of true facts that have the effect of attributing to the person attitudes or actions that are not accurate and that are objectionable to a reasonable person.

4. *Public disclosure of private facts about a person.* It is primarily this last type, the public disclosure of private facts, that is at issue in *Guinn* and other church discipline cases.[26]

TYPES OF INVASIONS OF PRIVACY

While the precise law regarding this type of invasion of privacy is still not altogether settled and may vary from state to state, there are some general summaries of the law that are helpful.

The Restatement (Second) of Torts, 652, adopted by Oklahoma, summarizes the law of invasion of privacy:

One who gives publicity to a matter concerning the private life of another is subject to liability to the other for invasion of his privacy, if the matter publicized is of a kind that (A) would be highly offensive to a reasonable person, and (B) is not of legitimate concern to the public.[27]

To make a case for invasion of privacy of this type, then, one must show that the defendant disclosed private information that a reasonable person of ordinary sensibilities would object to having made public. To summarize, the elements of any privacy action are the following:

Public disclosure . . .

There must be *publicity* given to the information; it must be communicated to others.

. . . *of private facts* . . .

The information made public must be *private*. If it is a matter of the public record or is already known to the public, then it is no longer private and there has been no invasion. "Therefore, to whatever degree and in whatever connection a man's life has ceased to be private . . . to that extent the protection of the right of privacy is withdrawn."[28]

There is no liability where the facts are on public record, such as birth and marriage records, military service records, court reports, tax delinquency records, death certificates, and the like.[29]

. . . which are objectionable to a reasonable person.

Not every "private" fact that is revealed subjects one to liability. The protections apply only to those facts whose revelation would be "highly offensive" to the reasonable person.

If a plaintiff can show these "elements," he has made what is called a *prima facie* case. It is then up to the defense to establish any justifications, excuses, or privileges. These defenses are quite important in invasion of privacy cases. What are some of the common defenses?

Not truth. We have seen that "truth" is an absolute defense to actions for defamation. However, one of the special "advantages" of suing for invasion of privacy, and one that surely the plaintiff recognized in *Guinn* and its successors, is that truth is usually taken for granted. To some extent truthfulness aggravates the invasion; someone has revealed a truth that was a secret.

Legitimate public interest and constitutional limits. When the information is of legitimate public interest (what is sometimes called "newsworthiness") it is usually not an invasion of privacy to publish it. The issues and cases often involve media accounts of private lives of persons. Consider the following cases and decisions.

In *Melvin v. Reid* the defendant made a motion picture in 1925, *The Red Kimono,* based on a true-life story using the woman's real maiden name and including true accounts of numerous unsavory aspects of her life as a prostitute; she had been tried but acquitted of murder. The behavior depicted in the movie had taken place seven years earlier, and the woman had since lived a normal and respectable life; her past was unknown to the community. The California court upheld her cause of action in a suit for invasion of privacy noting that she had changed her life and "should have been permitted to continue its course without having her reputation and social standing destroyed by the publication of the story of her former depravity with no excuse other than the expectation of private gain by the publishers." The court went on to note: "Even the thief on the cross was permitted to repent during the hours of his final agony."[30]

The opposite conclusion was reached in another famous case in New York, *Sidis v. F-R Publishing Corp.*, in which a magazine published an update story on a "young prodigy" who in the intervening years had lived a life of seclusion.[31] The article was an unfriendly one, "merciless in its dissection of intimate details of its subject's personal life,"[32] and Sidis sued. The court rejected the claim for invasion of privacy, however, concluding that even though years had intervened, Sidis was still a "public figure" and the public's interest in the news was paramount.

Here we see a tension between the right to be left alone and the public interest. Of course, concepts such as public interest and newsworthiness are rather elusive, and the press is eager to extend the newsworthiness concept as far as possible. Further, the public's "thirst for lurid details" may well run beyond legitimate public interest. When is there a legitimate public interest, as opposed to mere curiosity? Brandeis and Warren concluded that "the design of the law must be to protect those persons with whose affairs the community has no legitimate concern from being dragged into an undesirable and undesired publicity."[33]

The courts have increasingly granted a privilege under constitutional standards for reporting about the "private" lives of "public figures" who by virtue of their position, such as politicians and entertainment stars, have thrust themselves into the limelight. Occasionally even private figures who have become noteworthy are treated as if they were public figures, and the privilege extends to reporting about their private lives. But where do you draw the line? The constitutional issues emerge because of the court's commitment to what it has called an "uninhibited, robust and wide-open" discussion on public issues. In defamation actions, public figures may succeed only when they can show actual malice or a reckless disregard of truth.[34] Some of the same concern not to inhibit free speech in regard to public matters has been applied in invasion of privacy cases where courts have rejected suits when they have found a legitimate interest, and no showing of actual malice.[35]

Consent or waiver. Persons may, of course, waive their privacy or consent to its invasion. The most obvious example is a person who agrees to allow his name or picture to be used in advertising. However, the consent may be less specific than a formal contract. There are many ways one can agree to the disclosure of private facts, such as by filling out a credit application.

Qualified privilege of community of legitimate interest. One of the most controverted aspects of the *Guinn* case is whether or not under Oklahoma law there is a privilege that applies to the communication of private facts of a nature similar to that which applies to libel and slander, that is, when the communication is in good faith, without actual malice, and takes place between persons with a legitimate interest.

Marian's counsel argued in *Guinn* that the Oklahoma court should not recognize such a privilege and sought to discount cases the defendants relied upon: "The qualified privilege of libel and slander should not be applied to the very different tort of invasion of privacy."[36]

It is clear that many cases and legal commentators have held that such a privilege does exist. For example, in a Kansas case, *Munsell v. Ideal Food Stores,* the court accepted the rule that "the right of privacy does not prohibit the communication of any matter though of a private nature, when the publication is made under circumstances that would render it a privileged communication according to the law of libel and slander."[37] In a subsequent case, the Kansas Supreme Court concluded:

Concerning an action for invasion of privacy, based upon the communications of matters of a private nature, *Munsell* settled these principles— (1) a warranted invasion of privacy is not actionable; (2) *communication or publication of a matter under circumstances which would render it a privileged communication according to the law of libel and slander will not support an action*; and (3) generally, the issue whether a publication is qualifiedly privileged is a question of law to be determined by the court.[38]

Such a rule seems clearly required. If under defamation law good faith communications between persons with a legitimate interest are privileged even if untrue, it is incongruous to give them less protection when they are truthful and accurate. Further, the policy of recognizing that information is essential among communities of interest and that such persons should not be intimidated by civil tort liability from sharing information applies even more strongly to privacy claims than to defamation actions. If privacy claims are permitted under such circumstances, then good faith and even accurate judgments in disciplinary proceedings by all kinds of organizations will be conducted only at the risk of the financial destruction of the association and its leadership. It would act as an enormously effective barrier to communication, discourage integrity, and reward duplicity and silence in the face of immorality. Even former president Nixon might plead invasion!

How should this law, however unclear it may be, apply to church discipline cases like *Guinn*? In a legal context, the questions are these: (1) Has the defendant church legally invaded the plaintiff's privacy; that is, can the plaintiff prove that private facts were publicized in a manner that a reasonable person would object to? (2) If so, does the defendant have a defense that makes the invasion legally permissible? In most situations we have observed, we believe that the defendant-church has a strong case on both points. While the specific facts of any given case will necessarily affect the analysis, the pattern of cases suggests that the proper application of traditional legal tort and invasion of privacy principles should result in no liability for the church and a dismissal of such claims by the court.

APPLYING THESE PRINCIPLES TO CHURCH DISCIPLINE

THE BASIC ALLEGATION. Serious questions remain regarding whether or not plaintiffs can really make out their basic cases. The third element—offensiveness of publication to a reasonable person—need not be contested. We do not doubt that a reasonable person would object to the public revelation of Marian's conduct. The church would have no interest in denying that. From its perspective, the public revelation of sinful conduct ought to be something a person would object to at the purely human level, feeling embarrassed, guilty, exposed. Adam and Eve also sought to hide!

But the other two required elements are considerably less clear. First, certainly under the facts in *Guinn,* it may be argued that the revealed facts were not private but already public and that the church congregation was told nothing it did not already know from general talk about town. Aspects of the trial record seem to confirm that Marian's affair was well known. There were no allegations that the church went beyond what was apparently public knowledge nor that they had sought to expose intricate details of the affair; it was not an X-rated expose in living color. The church told the congregation nothing new.

Secondly, one might wonder whether in *Guinn* the defendant made any *public* disclosure. It was not the church that held press conferences, issued general news release, or commenced public legal action that brought Marian's story to the world. They kept the information within their own church family, and it is by no means clear that information shared within an associational or church body is "public." In a general sense, not everything told to a church body acting in formal session under its bylaws is construed as public information.

THE DEFENSE. Even if the basic elements of the plaintiff's case are assumed, the church has substantial defenses in any action for invasion of privacy. First, under the circumstances in *Guinn* a strong case can be made that Marian Guinn's church membership operated as a type of consent or waiver to communications of this sort and that the communication was warranted by the nature of the body to which she voluntarily attached herself.

Part of the character of any association is some waiver of privacy; one who joins chooses thereby to reveal certain things, to share relevant information and confidences. Depending on the nature of the organization this may be a rather deep and profound sharing, or slight, and may involve finances, personal affairs, or a wide variety of other private facts. Associations would be meaningless if they were a mere collection of individuals who refused to share or confide. This applies more strongly to the church. Its character is a body with emphases on mutuality and community. Its comprehensive nature touches the bases of our being and values and implies a level of sharing—of vulnerability—that exceeds any other association. It is more like a marriage than a club. It is biblically committed as a highly integrated body whose parts are mutually dependent in both joy and suffering. Duties arise out of that theology: duties of mutual care, confession, and self-revelation. Many of these elements in the life of the church assume and require a release of the tendency to hold back, store up, hide, and withdraw. To join is to release self-sufficiency. It is recognized that those who choose to enter into such a community are "letting go" of some of these human proclivities of self-protection in order to achieve the release and freedom of openness in a trusted community. One who enters such a fellowship cannot complain that the community so conducts its life. That is its character, its essence. When one says "I do" to the relationship of the body of Christ, one has invested in a covenant community that reshapes the "privacy" of autonomous life. One cannot have both community and autonomy. Brothers and sisters retain their individuality and an important measure of privacy, but it is limited by their relationship.

Despite the claims of the plaintiff, which regrettably succeeded at the trial court level, the qualified privilege of such communications within a community of interest seems clearly applicable to the church for all the same reasons noted above. Here is a community marked by mutual commitments, bound by their faith to one another. They are "one in the Spirit." Where, as in *Guinn,* the church's good faith is not even challenged and the relevance of the information to the church moral code is acknowledged, the privilege should apply. There clearly was a legitimate community of interest in the information communicated, and thus the communication of these private facts under these circumstances is not legally improper.

Finally, we believe there are fundamental First Amendment constitutional issues of free exercise of religion and the prohibition of government entanglement with religion that effectively bar such actions under the circumstances such as those concerning *Guinn.* We shall review those issues in a subsequent chapter.

CONCLUSION While the protections of privacy are legitimate concerns in both the political and social character of our society, any attempt to use such tools to penalize the conduct of the life of the church would seem inconsistent with the basic legal principles of such claims. In cases such as *Guinn* the plaintiff has a questionable case to begin with, and even if she establishes the elements of the *prima facie* case, the defenses of consent and qualified privilege ought, as a matter of law, to serve as a defense that permits the church to carry out its rights as both an association and as a religious community.

Plaintiffs who find themselves with no

claim under traditional associational or tort law such as defamation should not be permitted by the courts to fabricate a newly developing tort into an instrument to achieve indirectly what they could not do directly. It would be a genuine invasion of the privacy of the church to use privacy notions to hold it liable under the circumstances outlined here.

NOTES

[1]Cited by John H. F. Shattuck, *Rights of Privacy* (Skokie, Ill.: National Textbook Company, 1983), 1.

[2]Amended complaint, *Guinn v. Church of Christ of Collinsville* (hereinafter *Guinn v. Church*), No. 81-929 (Dist. Ct. Tulsa County, Okla., filed Nov. 23, 1981).

[3]*Shive v. Adkisson*, No. 84 CV 6646 (Denver County Ct., Colo., Oct.—, 1983).

[4]*Kelly v. Christian Community Church*, No. 545117 (Super. Ct. Santa Clara County, Cal., filed Mar. 22, 1984).

[5]*Galella v. Onassis*, 353 F. Supp. 196 (S.D. N.Y. 1972), *decree modified*, 487 F.2d 986 (2d Cir. 1973).

[6]*Daily-Times Democrat Co. v. Graham*, 276 Ala. 380, 162 So. 2d 474 (1964).

[7]*York v. Story*, 324 F.2d 450 (9th Cir. 1963).

[8]*Banks v. King Features Syndicate*, 30 F. Supp. 352 (S.D. N.Y. 1939).

[9]*Hamberger v. Eastman*, 106 N.H. 107, 206 A.2d 239 (1964).

[10]William Zelermyer, *Invasion of Privacy* (Syracuse, N.Y.: Syracuse University Press, 1956), 25.

[11]Clinton Rossiter, "The Pattern of Liberty in *Aspects of Liberty*," ed. Milton R. Konvitz and Clinton Rossiter (Ithaca, N.Y.: Johnson Repr., 1958), 15-17. The right to privacy has implications not simply for individuals but for groups, that is, the right of groups of persons to be free from the interference of government. "The interest protected by group privacy is the desire and need of people to come together, to exchange information, share feelings, make plans and act in concert to attain their objectives." Edward J. Bloustein, *Individual and Group Privacy* (New Brunswick, N.J.: Transaction Books, 1978), 125. The premise of giving up total privacy in the mutual

sharing of the group is the expectation that what is shared there is not public. Such protections of group privacy may have very important implications for religious liberty.

Protections of group privacy—their mail lists, memberships, etc.—have been subject to several court tests. In a seminal case the Supreme Court struck down an Alabama statute that required the NAACP to provide the state with a list of its members, noting the potential for reprisals and "manifestations of public hostility." *NAACP v. Alabama,* 357 U.S. 449, 461 (1958). In another case, the Court also noted that "compelled disclosure . . . [of memberships] can seriously infringe on privacy of association and belief guaranteed by the First Amendment." *Buckley v. Valeo,* 424 U.S. 1, 64 (1976), upholding the Federal Election Campaign Act's disclosure requirements.

[12]Alan Westin, *Privacy and Freedom* (New York: Atheneum, 1970), 33.

[13]Ibid., 34.

[14]Leontine Young, *Life Among the Giants* (New York: McGraw-Hill, 1966), cited in Westin, *Privacy and Freedom,* 34.

[15]Karen Horney, *Our Inner Conflicts* (New York: Norton, 1945), 76. See also Freida Fromm-Reichmann, "Loneliness," *Psychiatry* 22 (1959), 2, 3.

[16]It does seem that someone might try to develop a theology of privacy, balancing biblical interests in autonomy, uniqueness with revelation, community, and how privacy (social, psychological, political) fits

[17]Joseph Story, *Commentaries on the Constitution of the United States,* vol. 2, 2nd ed. (Boston: Little & Brown, 1851), 591, 597, 600.

[18]Ibid., 608.

[19]*Commonwealth v. Lovett,* 4 Clark 5 (Pa. 1831).

[20]Warren and Brandeis, "The Right of Privacy," 4 *Harv. L. Rev.,* 193, 196 (1890).

[21]Zelermyer, 25. One commentator declared that the article "enjoys the unique distinction of having synthesized at one stroke a whole new category of legal rights and of having initiated a new field of jurisprudence." Annot., 57 A.L.R.3d 16 (1974). One of the foremost critics of the legal theory of invasion of privacy has been Harry Kalven, Jr., who criticized the whole concept and Prosser's analysis in "Privacy in Tort Law—Were Warren and Brandeis Wrong?" 31 *Law and Contemp. Prob.,* 327

(1966). As to the tort of public disclosure of private facts, Kalven insisted, "To begin with, the tort has no legal profile. We do not know what constitutes a prima facie case, we do not know on what basis damages are to be measured. . . . The problem of definition then is to state what less than every such unconsented-to reference is prima facie tortious. . . . The lack of legal profile and the enormity of the counterprivilege converge to raise for me the question whether privacy is really a viable tort remedy. The mountain, I suggest, has brought forth a pretty small mouse . . ." (Prosser, 333, 337).

[22]*Roberson v. Rochester Folding Box Co.,* 64 N.E. 442, 443 (1902).

[23]Ibid. The Court observed: "The courts, however, being without authority to legislate, are required to decide cases upon principle, and so are necessarily embarrassed by precedents created by an extreme and therefore, unjustifiable, application of an old principle."

[24]The Supreme Court in 1965 took a major step in enunciating a constitutional doctrine of a right of privacy, the notion that certain governmental actions are constitutionally impermissible because they interfere with a fundamental constitutional liberty of privacy. In *Griswold v. Connecticut,* the Court held 7-2 that a Connecticut law forbidding the distribution of birth control information was a violation of a right to marital privacy. The opinion of the Court, written by Justice Douglas, spoke of the "zones of privacy" that are created by various constitutional concepts. Justice Goldberg, writing for himself, was joined by Justices Warren and Brennan in declaring that the right of privacy is "so rooted in the tradition and conscience of our people as to be ranked as fundamental." Goldberg insisted that privacy was a "fundamental" personal liberty "retained by the people." Justice Stewart in his dissent agreed that the Connecticut law was "uncommonly silly" but declared he could "find no such general right of privacy" in the Constitution or in prior decisions. In a more disturbing ruling grounded in these rights of privacy, the Supreme Court in the major abortion decision, *Roe v. Wade,* 410 U.S. 113 (1973), struck down abortion restrictions as an unconstitutional interference with the right of privacy. Other courts have used concepts of constitutionally based privacy to uphold the right of unmarried cohabitation (*Ravin v. State,* 537 P.2d. 494 Alaska [1975]), and in the famous Karen Quinlan case, to permit an incompetent dependent to die (*In re Quinlan,* 70 N.J. 10, 355 A.2d. 647 [1976]).

[25]Prosser set forth his legal theories about invasion of privacy issues in a highly influential article, "Privacy," 48 *Cal. L. Rev.* 383 (1960).

[26]Conceivably the "intrusive" type could also be an issue where church officials were "investigating" conduct, and, of course, "false light" could emerge where a church in its publication created an impression that was false and objectionable.

[27]*McCormack v. Oklahoma Publishing Company,* 613 P.2d 737 (Okla. 1980); *Munley v. ISC Financial House, Inc.,* 584 P.2d 1336 (Okla. 1978).

[28]*Gill v. Hearst Publishing Co.,* 40 Cal. 2d 224, 253 P.2d 441 (1953); *Metter v. Los Angeles Examiner,* 35 Cal. App. 2d 304, 95 P.2d 491 (1939); *Cabaniss v. Hipsley,* 114 Ga. App. 367, 151 S.E.2d 496 (1966); *Hurley v. Northwest Publications, Inc.,* 273 F. Supp. 967, aff'd 398 F.2d 346 (8th Cir. 1967); *Raynor v. American Broadcasting Co.,* 222 F. Supp. 795 (D.C. Pa. 1963).

[29]See *Cox Broadcasting v. Cohn,* 420 U.S. 469 (1975), where the court held that publishing truthful information from a public record was constitutionally protected in spite of a state law that made it a crime to publish the name of a rape victim. Here the name had been disclosed in court proceedings and had appeared in judicial records open to public inspection.

[30]*Melvin v. Reid,* 112 Cal. App. 285, 297 Pa. 91 (Dist. Ct. App. 1931).

[31]*Sidis v. F-R Publishing Corp.,* 113 F.2d 806 (1940).

[32]113 F.2d 807 (1940).

[33]Warren and Brandeis, *supra* note 18, at 414, 415.

[34]*N.Y. Times v. Sullivan,* 376 U.S. 254, 84 S. Ct. 710 (1964).

[35]*Time v. Hill,* 385 U.S. 374 (1967); *Gertz v. Robert Welch, Inc.,* 418 U.S. 323 (1974); *Cox Broadcasting Corp. v. Cohn,* 420 U.S. 469 (1975).

[36]Plaintiff's Brief in Response to Defendant's Motion for Summary Judgment, *Guinn v. Church* (filed Aug. 27, 1982).

[37]*Munsell v. Ideal Food Stores,* 494 P.2d 1063, 1075 (Kans. 1972).

[38]*Senogles v. Security Benefit Life Ins. Co.,* 536 P.2d 1358, 1362 (Kans. 1975) (emphasis added).

9 OUTRAGEOUS!

> ... the very capacity for experiencing shame, the design of shame is inscribed in the human soul.... This is the *sine qua non* of humanity.
> *Eric Heller*

> But what if, contrary to what is now so generally assumed, shame is natural to man? ... What if it is shamelessness that is unnatural....
> *Walter Berns*[1]

Which is "outrageous"? Select one option below:

1. A mother of small children carrying on an affair with a man.
2. A church that dismisses and disciplines a woman carrying on such an affair.

It is clear that for plaintiffs such as Marian Guinn the answer is number two. A church that chooses to call its members to account and expresses its moral judgments within its community is seen as outrageous.

The plaintiffs all seem to agree, and it doesn't take a legal scholar to see a pattern in these church discipline lawsuits. The allegations in the complaints sound as if they had been generated by the same word processor. Note some examples from several complaints.[2]

Marian Guinn's complaint alleges that

the publication of statements about the plaintiff
. . . was conduct which was and is *extreme and
outrageous* and which intentionally and recklessly
caused *severe emotional distress* to plaintiff.

James Shive's fourteenth claim for relief alleges that in his case the publication

was and is *extreme and outrageous* and which intentionally and recklessly caused *severe emotional
distress* to the plaintiff James L. Shive. . . . The
acts . . . were so *extreme and outrageous,* willful,
wanton and oppressive and were made under circumstances with malice and insult and a wanton
and reckless disregard of the plaintiff James L.
Shive's rights and feelings.

John R. Kelly alleges that

the actions of the defendants . . . constitute *outrageous* conduct which is not privileged and was
likely to cause plaintiff *emotional distress.* . . . The
acts of defendants . . . were willful, fraudulent,
malicious, and oppressive and with conscious disregard of plaintiff's rights with the intent to vex,
annoy, harass, and injure plaintiff. . . .

Charles Roberson complained

that the actions of the defendants . . . constitute
outrageous conduct which is not privileged and
was likely to cause plaintiff *emotional distress* and
suffering [and that] . . . the acts of defendants . . .
were willful, fraudulent, malicious, and oppressive, and with conscious disregard of plaintiff's
rights, with the intent to vex, annoy, harass, and
injure plaintiff and in fact did cause plaintiff to
suffer fright, nervousness, grief, anxiety, embarrassment, apprehension, and terror. . . .

There does seem to be a pattern in these
complaints! Why the similarity? Why do they
all speak of "outrageous" conduct?

The reason is they are all using the magic
legal words to try and make out a case that

THE INFLICTION OF EMOTIONAL DISTRESS

the defendant church and its leaders are liable for the intentional infliction of emotional distress. This tort, like the invasion of privacy complaint, is relatively modern. And like the invasion of privacy claim, it provides a potential for an end run around the defense of truth. This is made easier because it is vague and open to a range of interpretation. In short, it is an ideal type of claim for persons aggrieved by truthful charges in church discipline cases.

The courts have been slow to recognize claims for the infliction of emotional distress. This is largely because of concern over issues, the problem of proving emotional or mental distress when there is no physical harm, and the danger of malicious and frivolous suits. Prosser, the torts legal scholar, endorsed early objections that the tort was "too subtle and speculative" and failed to specify the character of the injury. He observed that the action was "so evanescent, intangible, peculiar and variable with individuals as to be beyond anticipation or prediction."[3]

It also has been widely recognized that civil law was never intended to provide a legal remedy for all discomfort. As a comment to the Restatement (Second) of Torts noted, "There is no occasion for the law to intervene in every case where someone's feelings are hurt."[4]

Historically, courts have granted damages for mental distress and suffering when it was an incident to bodily injury (e.g., pain and suffering awards in medical malpractice cases). Also, in some specialized situations awards for mental distress have been given even without physical injury, as in cases of assault and false imprisonment. However, there was never a remedy for mental distress alone.

Today courts have increasingly provided a remedy for emotional distress under certain narrow conditions where the acts of the defendant are so "outrageous" as to overcome the reluctance to entertain such claims and where the victim has as a result suffered severe emotional distress.

The English case that "broke through the shackles of the older law" was *Wilkinson v. Downton* in which a practical joker told a woman her husband had been smashed up in an accident and was lying with both legs broken.[5] He told her she was to take two pillows and go at once in a cab to bring him home. The shock to her nervous system produced serious and permanent physical consequences. In the light of the facts in this case "the enormity of the outrage overthrew the settled rule of law."[6]

The cases in which liability has been found for infliction of emotional distress illustrate the kind of outrageous conduct normally required: institutionalizing a woman suspected of insanity through a concocted tale of an injured husband and child,[7] spreading false rumors of a son's hanging himself,[8] bringing a mob to the plaintiff's door with a threat to lynch him unless he leaves town,[9] wrapping up a gory dead rat instead of the loaf of bread a woman had ordered,[10] and bullying a schoolgirl with threats of public disgrace and prison unless she signs a confession of immoral conduct.[11]

Liability has also been found, and at times more easily, in cases involving extreme and harassing methods employed by bill collectors, insurance adjustors, and other similar creditors.[12] Public carriers are also under a higher duty, and even a gross insult may be sufficient to trigger liability in such cases. In one case, an employee of a carrier was held liable for referring to a woman passenger as "a big fat woman like you."[13]

Where persons know of the special vulnerability of individuals, less extreme conduct may cause liability, as with children,[14] sick persons, or pregnant women.[15] In one famous Louisiana case, the defendants buried a "pot of gold" for an eccentric and mentally infirm old maid to "find," and when she did, they escorted her in triumph to the city hall where she opened it in public, suffering great humiliation.[16]

In Oklahoma, where *Guinn* was decided, a cause of action for intentional infliction of emotional distress has been recognized. In the *Breeden*[17] case the Oklahoma Supreme Court adopted the statement of the law regarding this type of claim as set forth in the Restatement (Second) of Torts Section 46 (1965). That section summarizes the law as it exists in most states as follows:

§ 46 Outrageous Conduct Causing Emotional Distress

(1) One who by extreme and outrageous conduct intentionally or recklessly causes severe emotional distress to another is subject to liability for such emotional distress, and if bodily harm to the other results from it, [is subject to liability] for such bodily harm.

Comment 1 to that section provides in part:

Liability has been found only where the conduct has been so outrageous in character, and so extreme in degree, as to go beyond all possible bounds of decency, and to be regarded as atrocious, and utterly intolerable in a civilized community. Generally, the case is one in which a recitation of the facts of an average member of the community would arouse his resentment against the actor, and lead him to exclaim, "Outrageous!"

While the Oklahoma cases finding liability for emotional distress are relatively few, they illustrate the nature of the action. In one case the defendant in a dispute over a payment on a TV set threatened to kill the dogs at the plaintiff's house and banged on all doors and windows, lunging at the front door trying to break in.[18] In a second case, a bank officer threatened to ruin the plaintiff's credit and made threatening phone calls over a debt of the plaintiff's son.[19] A threat to publicize nude photographs and tape of lovemaking unless a lien was released was held to be sufficiently outrageous conduct in a third case.[20]

These cases teach that in almost any jurisdiction, according to the nature of an action for the infliction of emotional distress, the plaintiff must show by the preponderance of the evidence the following elements to make out a *prima facie* case: (1) An act of the defendant that is "extreme and outrageous" (2) that is done with the intent of inflicting emotional or mental distress,[21] and (3) that the act is the actual cause of (4) severe emotional distress.

EXTREME AND OUTRAGEOUS. In order to minimize frivolous actions and assure that legal remedies are available only in appropriate cases, the plaintiff must show not merely that there is some emotional distress but that it arises from acts of the defendant that are "extreme" and "outrageous." These are acts so offensive that the community would rise up and condemn them as beyond the bounds of decency. One must prove more than bad judgment or hurt feelings. He must prove the defendant's actions were "beyond all bounds of decency" so as to be regarded as "atrocious" and "utterly intolerable."[22]

That is a very demanding standard, and intentionally so. How could Marian Guinn's counsel establish such a level of conduct by the church elders? They attempted to demonstrate (and the jury apparently found) that the persistence of the elders in "going forward" after Marian had told them she did not want to consult with them was "extreme and outrageous." In their brief, Marian's attorneys cited newspaper letters attacking the church as evidence of the "outrage" of the community.[23]

If that seems unconvincing of "extreme and outrageous" conduct, one can understand concerns about the fickleness of juries entrusted with evaluating religious conduct. The key issue rests here on the standard of "outrageousness." We suppose one might make a case that in some sense the church "intended" Marian to feel distressed, and that she did suffer distress. But unless one can show that the action of the elders was "extreme and outrageous" there is no liability. Former President Nixon was distressed, deeply so, but there is no liability because the actions of the Watergate Commission and others who accused him were not extreme and outrageous but rather expressions of proper indignation and judgment.

It is also most likely that if a judge or jury believes the actions of a defendant are in fact extreme, outrageous, and beyond decency, then it will be easier to "prove" elements of intent, causation, and damages.

But is it extreme and outrageous for a church to advise its members of the dismissal of another person and the reasons for that action? Is it beyond the bounds of decency for a church to hold and consistently carry out the view that the body of believers is such a community that their obligations toward one another include those of correction and discipline? Are the clear biblical mandates practiced by many religious communities now indecent under the law?

INTENT. Did the elders of the Collinsville church "intend" to inflict emotional distress on Marian? According to Marian's counsel, their "intent" is proved because there is "no question" that the church elders knew that publication of these matters concerning Marian's private life would "emotionally upset her and cause her emotional distress" and that Marian had in fact so informed them in her letter of September 24.

"Intentional" conduct requires intent to inflict emotional distress in at least one of three senses: first, and most commonly, a deliberate intent and desire to cause it; second, knowledge that certain consequences were substantially certain to occur if someone did certain things; and a few courts add a third, a willful, wanton, and reckless disregard of the consequences where there is a high probability that harm will occur. For example, if I shoot a gun into a crowd I may not actually intend to hurt anyone, but I will be held to have legal "intent." (In one case where "intent" was found, a person took a very badly injured man home to his pregnant wife without warning.[24])

In *Guinn* there is not the slightest evidence that the elders at Collinsville "intended" anything other than to bring Marian Guinn back into the life of the church. Their basic intent was certainly to be restorative, to protect the remaining community of faith, to guard the moral life of the church, and supremely to be obedient to the biblical vision of the character and duty of the church. The mere fact that their acts were willful (as opposed to unconscious, autonomic) does not create the kind of "intent" normally required for such a tort; the type of intent found in the case law is that of the malicious prankster or harasser.

One might argue that an aspect of the intent of the church was to put Marian in a place where the reality of her sin pressed in upon her making her recognize the separateness from the community that sin brings. And such a sense would be a type of emotional distress. But the mere fact that they knew she would be in such distress would not seem adequate to sustain the action.

CAUSATION. It is necessary for the plaintiff to show that the actions of the defendant were the cause of the harm—the mental distress. As we shall note later, one might ask in a theological and psychological frame of reference whether or not the church's acts are the real cause of Marian's distress.

What is "emotional distress"? Prosser says, "It includes all highly unpleasurable mental reactions, such as fright, horror, grief, shame, humiliation, anger, embarrassment, chagrin, disappointment, worry and nausea."[25] It is not enough, as we have seen, to show that one is upset. Usually what must be shown is a severity of such distress: "The emotional distress must in fact exist, and it must be severe."[26]

Here also the courts seek to limit actions so that the law does not become a wheel to smooth all the rough edges of life.

Did Marian and others in these suits suffer? Doubtless they did. One cannot be part of church discipline, be involved in the activities noted in the cases, without a heavy emotional investment. It may have been severe, and churches need not challenge the claim that these plaintiffs suffer greatly. Although we may challenge their allegations that church discipline is the fundamental cause, we don't deny their suffering.

In addition to challenging or denying the basic allegations of "extreme and outrageous" conduct, necessary willful intent, causation, and damages, the defendant church and its leaders are fully entitled to raise affirmative defenses. We have noted these previously, such as waiver (by joining a community with moral commitments and community priorities persons submit themselves thereby to the moral judgments of that community and to its discipline), privilege (sharing within the community such information as is of legitimate interest to that community), and the constitutional defenses of free exercise and establishment. We shall not review those again here, for the basic nature of the defense is the same as already has been discussed.

THE DEFENSE AND SOCIETY'S TRENDS

The allegations of emotional distress may be the most troubling of all the aspects of these lawsuits, for they reflect particularly disturbing trends.

The claim that the church has acted "beyond the bounds of decency" is both shocking and ironic. It is ironic that conduct that would have been "outrageous" a few years ago—that is, Marian's affair—now is apparently not shocking at all; and what now is allegedly outrageous and indecent is a church exercising church discipline in regard to such moral conduct.

Two options exist to explain verdicts such as *Guinn*. One is that this jury is an anomaly that made a strange and bizarre decision—a glitch in the moral framework of the community in Collinsville. Or alternatively, the *Guinn* decision accurately, albeit tragically, reflects the upside-down moral world in

which the church seems to be living, under
the "new rules" that Yankelovich said are
dominating American culture.[27] In this topsy-
turvy moral universe it is the moral purist,
the one who expects fidelity and moral integrity, who creates dissonance and who is
judged. He is the one who is so "out of
touch" that his very demands are labeled
"outrageous." One is reminded of the reversed reality, the "doublethink," of Orwell's
1984. In such a world it was possible

to know and not to know, to be conscious of complete truthfulness while telling carefully con-
structed lies, to hold simultaneously two opinions
. . . to use logic against logic, to repudiate morality while laying claim to it.

Everything becomes its opposite. The war
agency is the Ministry of Peace, and the
Nazi-like police agencies are directed by the
Ministry of Love.[28]

Orwell is too close for comfort to the truth.
In *Guinn*, this prophecy that "morality"
would be the basis for an assault upon morality itself has come to pass. In the requirement that conduct be "outrageous" and
"beyond the bounds of decency" we see
moral notions, and yet precisely these concepts are used to attack those who speak for
morality. Decency is indecent; indecency is
decent!

In such a society religion is submitted to
the psychologists and mental health professionals who will tell us what they perceive is
"healthy," "functional," "enabling," and
"fulfilling of human potential." All other religious views will be "unhealthy," "counterproductive," and subject to "treatment."
Perhaps, as in the Soviet Union, we can send
such "sick" people as the elders at Collinsville to psychiatric hospitals where they can

be "cured" so that they fit better into the community of "live and let live."

The decision also reflects the dangers of relying on juries to assess the appropriateness of religious doctrines and moral factors.[29] If religion is to be judged by contemporary moral standards, then many faiths, including that of evangelicals and Catholics—indeed all moral orthodoxy—will be seen as archaic and "outrageous." If religion is "outrageous," it is not entitled to the respect and protection of the law. Recent cases in the United States have reflected the tendency of juries to spin out huge damage awards against unpopular religious views. In Oregon, a jury awarded $2 million to a woman who withdrew from the Scientologists; she alleged their promises of a better life for her were fraudulent. That decision was overturned, and in 1985 a jury again awarded the plaintiff money damages, this time $39 million! Interviews with jurors in the "clergy malpractice" suit against John MacArthur and Grace Community Church reportedly showed some jurors were siding with the plaintiffs because they felt the church was too narrow or strict. Such judgments by jurors reflect the dangers of turning over to them the liberties of conscience and religious life that must flourish not only when popularly hailed but when rejected as well.

Are we going to insist that religion "fit" the cultural mores of the community? Must its moral principles conform to those of potential juries? If it conducts its affairs with religious integrity and internal consistency and in keeping with a dominant strand of Christian history but is out of touch with contemporary moral views, must it pay "punitive damages"?

Possibly, the church's actions were viewed with abhorrence by the community because

there was an implicit judgment in its moral
views of the life-style that has come to domi-
nate so much of American life. The Solzhen-
itsyns, the biblical prophets, will always be
labeled, tarred and feathered, and written
off, if not persecuted, because their moral
commitments are a constant reproach to the
amorality of the societies in which they live.
It has always been so! Were the jury members merely voting for their own moral
views, for their own right to be free of such
judgments in their churches?

One wonders how many other principles of
the church will be labeled as outrageous by a
society that has lost its moral roots. Other
convictions in jeopardy might be the
church's historic and biblical condemnation
of homosexual conduct, premarital sex, and
abortion on demand.

THE GIFT OF SHAME

A sense of shame is a lovely sign in a man.
Whoever has a sense of shame will not sin so
quickly; but whoever shows no sense of shame in
his visage, his father surely never stood on Mount
Sinai.
Talmud[30]

Of course, one need not doubt that Marian
and those similarly situated experience intense "mental distress." Accepting Prosser's
list of examples they also may have experienced "shame" or "embarrassment." But a
couple of questions are relevant: What is the
real cause of the shame? Is it the action of
the church? Isn't it rather the conduct of the
parties themselves that, now being brought
to light, reveals their conduct for what it truly is? Unlike typical emotional distress cases,
it is not really the conduct of the church—
reading letters, voting to expel—that produces the shame. It is rather the revelation
of what is hidden, the exposure. This is not a
case of a malicious, evil actor taunting the

innocent plaintiff, threatening, putting the person in fear. It is rather a defendant who has told the truth. The consequences were inevitable: "Be sure your sin will find you out," for, "whatsoever a man soweth, that shall he also reap" (Num. 32:23; Gal. 6:7).

Nixon no doubt felt mental anguish at Watergate's revelations. But the mental distress was of his own making. The revelation may have been the catalyst, but not the cause. It was only like turning on a light in a room. We insist it was the "sin" that created the distress.

The second question: Under certain circumstances, aren't shame and embarrassment a gift? They are kinds of mental distress that are really signs of our moral accountability, gifts of our conscience, incidents of our humanity.

Carl Schneider writes in *Shame, Exposure and Privacy* of the central role of shame in human experience, and insists, unlike those who would "dismiss it as a mechanism that is crippling or inhibiting" or an "obstacle to be overcome," that it is "a mark of our humanity."[31]

The great Russian nineteenth-century philosopher Vladimir Soloviev declared, "The feeling of shame is a fact which absolutely distinguishes man from all lower nature. . . . [It] is the true spiritual root of all human good and the distinctive characteristic of man as a moral being."[32]

SHAME AND CONSCIENCE.

Let shame then be defined as a kind of pain or uneasiness in respect of misdeeds past, present, or future, which seem to bring dishonour. . . .
Aristotle[33]

Shame is a central aspect of biblical thought and the sinner's response to his awareness of sin in the face of holiness, of infidelity in the face of covenant. See, for example, Ezra 9:6, 7 (JB): "My God, I am ashamed, I blush to lift my face to you, my God. For our crimes have increased, until they are higher than our heads, and our sin has piled up to heaven."

C. S. Lewis has a powerful passage on the tragedy of shame:

In the end that Face which is the delight or the terror of the universe must be turned upon each of us either with one expression or with the other, either conferring glory inexpressible or inflicting shame that can never be cured or disguised.[34]

The biblical witness is not alone. Schneider correctly, we think, notes, "Shame raises consciousness. Shame is the partner of value awareness; its very occurrence arises from the fact that we are *valuing* animals. . . . To extirpate shame is to cripple our humanity."[35] Indeed, a number of commentators have suggested that the rush to do away with shame is part of modern man's illusions, narcissism, and escape from the realities of evil, sin, and judgment. Peter Marin, writing in *Harpers* magazine on the est movement and philosophy, observed:

It is all so simple. . . . It has all the terrifying simplicity of the lobotomized mind: all complexity gone, and in its place the warm wind of forced simplicity blowing away the tag ends of conscience and shame.[36]

Schneider has caught the relationship between shame and conscience and the necessity of such inner claims to integrity:

When experience is viewed only in terms of the desire to eliminate restraint, judgment is necessarily warped. From such a perspective, shame stands condemned as "restrictive," or worse, "repressive." The falseness of this position is its refusal to recognize its own restrictiveness and repression.

What are restricted and denied are feelings of uneasiness, of reticence—feelings inchoate enough not to be able to claim the public stage, yet nonetheless valuable for their private character. Such feelings can be overridden, discounted or ignored only at a marked cost both to the individual and to society.[37]

Helen Merrell Lynd suggests that public exposure is only part of the dimension of shame. ". . . I think that this public exposure of even a private part of one's physical or mental character could not in itself have brought about shame unless one had already felt within oneself, not only dislike, but shame for these traits."[38]

Blushing, often a physiological manifestation of shame and embarrassment, has been itself a subject of fascinating studies. Nietzsche even declared that "man is the creature who blushes." Thomas Burgess, member of the Royal College of Surgeons, published an essay in 1839 entitled *The Physiology or Mechanism of Blushing*. Linking the "tint to the cheek" to "what is going on internally in the moral sanctuary," he suggested the entire phenomenon had a providential design so that our fellowman might know "whenever we transgressed or violated those rules which should be held sacred."[39]

SHAME AND SELF-DISCOVERY. The very idea of shame is exposure, uncovering; it is the Indo-European root of our word meaning "to cover." Shame is linked etymologically to the need for cover for that which is exposed; the biblical account of Genesis and the nakedness of Adam and Eve speak of the same human sense.

It is in the sense of shame that we know

ourselves, that "revelation" both from within and without is made known. The aspect of discovery is illustrated in this observation about shame by Kurt Riezler:

You are confronted with your own meanness. Your image of yourself is broken. You despise yourself. You will hate the man who puts you to shame. This hate is the most bitter of all, the most difficult to heal. It has the longest memory. Shame burns. Perhaps decades later you will suddenly remember and blush.[40]

Helen Merrell Lynd makes the same arresting point. "Shame interrupts any unquestioning, unaware sense of ourselves. . . . Fully faced, shame may become not primarily something to be covered, but a positive experience of revelation."[41]

It is not the presence of shame, but the absence of it that is tragic (Zeph. 3:5, "The unjust knoweth no shame").

Sartre describes shame in the imagery of a voyeur. "I have just glued my ear to the door and looked through a keyhole. I am alone. . . . But all of a sudden I hear footsteps in the hall. Someone is looking at me!"[42] "Through shame I have discovered an aspect of my being . . . I recognize that I am as the Other sees me."[43] Schneider on this aspect suggests:

The relational aspect of shame —the disorientation, the unexpected, painful self-consciousness— give shame this revelatory potential. They make self-confrontation inescapable. Normally, the self refuses to see itself; it looks away; it hides from itself. To know one's self is *painful*. There is much that, left to ourselves, we would just as soon overlook.[44]

If shame and embarrassment often function as marks of our humanity, revealing our own failures and calling us to integrity, we ought not to rush to judgment against those whose moral advocacy and expectations create the conditions in which conscience judges our lives. Certainly there is a kind of emotional distress that is destructive of human life and sensitivities, that debilitates and drains. But not all mental distress is of this brand. Perhaps to the extent that the elders have awakened in Marian a sense of emotional distress it has been precisely the kind that is a gift. It may be the kind that assumes her moral capacity and refuses to let her escape. Perhaps those who would let her escape that kind of distress are her greatest enemies.

CONCLUSION

The decision of the court to submit the issue of "extreme and outrageous conduct" on the part of the church to the jury and the jury's finding that such conduct existed represent a sad and ironic witness to the demise of moral principle and the ascendancy of relative values.

While we hope that Oklahoma appellate courts will apply proper legal principles and reverse the trial court's decisions in this regard, the "sense" of the jury and local court reflects an ominous trend.

Ideally, the values of the jury would have been such that the action of the church would in no way have been seen as peculiar, much less the sort Prosser said would cause a community to rise up and exclaim "Outrageous!" If not, then at least they might have decided that on religious liberty grounds the church ought not to be penalized for its moral commitments even if perceived as quaint. But they did neither—and therein lies a tragedy that speaks more sadly of our culture than it does of the damages to the Collinsville Church of Christ.

NOTES

[1]Walter Berns, "Pornography v. Democracy—A Case for Censorship," 22 *The Public Interest*, 3, 44 (Winter 1971).

[2]Emphases added.

[3]Prosser, "Insult and Outrage," 44 *Cal. L. Rev.* 40, 40-43 (1956). An early influential article on the subject was by Magruder, "Mental and Emotional Disturbance in the Law of Torts," 49 *Harv. L. Rev.* 1033 (1936). It noted concern about opening up a "wide vista of litigation in the field of bad manners" and suggested it would be quixotic of the law to try to provide a means of attempting to secure peace of mind.

[4]The Oklahoma Supreme Court itself had declared in *Munley v. ISC Financial House, Inc.*, "There is simply no room in the framework of our society for permitting one party to sue on the event of every intrusion into the psychic tranquility of an individual," 584 P.2d 1336, 1338 (Okla. 1978).

[5]*Wilkinson v. Downton*, 2 Q.B. 597 (1897).

[6]William Prosser, *The Law of Torts*, 4th ed. (St. Paul, Minn.: West Publishing, 1971), 55.

[7]*Savage v. Boies*, 77 Ark. 355, 272 P.2d 349 (1954).

[8]*Bielitski v. Obadiak*, 61 Dom. L. Rep. 494 (1921).

[9]*Wilson v. Wilkins*, 181 Ark. 137, 25 S.W.2d 428 (1930).

[10]*Great A & P Tea Co. v. Roch*, 160 Md. 189, 153A. 22 (1930).

[11]*Johnson v. Sampson*, 167 Minn. 203, 208 N.W. 814 (1926).

[12]In many states, the plaintiff need not show extreme and outrageous conduct to prevail against bill collectors. Even negligence may suffice in some states. For an analysis of these cases see Note, "Intentional Infliction of Mental Distress in the Debtor-Creditor Relationship," 37 *Albany L. Rev.* 797 (1973).

[13]*Haile v. New Orleans Ry & Light Co.*, 135 La. 229, 65 So. 225 (1914).

[14]The use of profane and obscene language in the presence of a ten-year-old child was the basis of recovery by the child, but the father, accustomed to such language, was not allowed to recover. *Fort Worth & Rio Grande R. Co. v. Bryant*, 210 S.W. 556 (Tex. Civ. App. 1919).

[15] A creditor came to the house of a woman seven months pregnant and screamed profanity, abuse, and accusations of dishonesty at her in the presence of others, as a result of which she suffered mental distress and a miscarriage. The court held in her favor. *Kirby v. Jules Chain Stores Co.*, 210 N.C. 808, 188 S.E. 625 (1936).

[16]*Nickerson v. Hodges*, 146 La. 735, 84 So. 37 (1920).

[17]*Breeden v. League Services Corp.*, 575 P.2d 1374 (Okla. 1978).

[18]*Reeves v. Melton*, 518 P.2d 57 (Okla. App. 1974).

[19]*Bennett v. City National Bank and Trust Co.*, 549 P.2d 393 (Okla. App. 1976).

[20]*Floyd v. Dodson*, 55 Okla. B.J. 44, 2480 (Nov. 27, 1984).

[21]Under some circumstances and jurisdictions, an action for *negligent* infliction of emotional distress may also be entertained. In such cases, the nature of the *intent* is substantially different.

[22]The attorney for the elders in *Guinn* argued that where the publication allegedly creating the emotional distress arose in the context of a qualified privilege, it could not be said to be "outrageous in character." He cited the *Breeden* case to the effect that where reasonable persons would disagree as to whether or not the conduct was outrageous, the standard of proof for outrageousness had not been met. The very existence of the privilege negated the required degree of "utter intolerableness" that is the basis for emotional distress actions.

[23]If community "outrage" is sufficient, religious liberty itself would be in deep trouble. People have at various points in history been outraged by integration, civil rights, democracy, and even Jesus. The law is not a tool for enforcing public prejudice.

[24]*Price v. Yellow Pine Paper Mill Co.*, 240 S.W. 588 (Tex. Civ. App. 1922).

[25]Prosser, "Insult and Outrage," 43.

[26]Prosser, *Torts*, 59.

[27]Daniel Yankelovich, *New Rules: Searching for Self-fulfillment in a World Turned Upside Down* (New York: Random House, 1981).

[28]The relevance of Orwell for contemporary society and issues of liberty has been reviewed in an article by Robert L. Toms, "Lessons from the Prophets Orwell and Paul for 1984," *Quarterly* 5, no. 1 (1984), 10.

[29]In Oklahoma, as set forth by its Supreme Court in *Breeden* (see note 17), it is the court's and not the jury's task to first "determine whether the defendant's conduct may reasonably be regarded as so extreme and outrageous as to permit recovery," and only where reasonable persons could disagree should the issue be given to the jury to decide. This is an important point. Where the court has the duty of first finding that at least some reasonable persons might hold the conduct was sufficiently outrageous, the court can prevent vindictive juries from using their powers to punish merely unpopular ideas. The role of the court is not simply to provide a vehicle for prejudice through civil suits but to assure that any alleged conduct could be found to be sufficiently extreme and outrageous.

[30]Cited by Carl Schneider, *Shame, Exposure and Privacy* (Boston: Beacon Press, 1977), 109.

[31]Ibid., 9, 13-15. Kate Millet, writing in *Ms.* (Forum: "The Shame Is Over," 1975, 27-29) insists that shame is the "absolute confirmation of 'older notions and values and moralities,'" and that we are to live "life against shame." Fritz Perls, the founder of Gestalt Therapy, declared: "I have called shame and embarrassment Quislings of the organism. . . . Shame, embarrassment, self-consciousness and fear restrict the individual's expressions." F. S. Perls, *Ego, Hunger and Aggression* (New York: Random House, 1969), 178.

[32]Cited by Schneider, 5.

[33]Aristotle, *Art of Rhetoric,* trans. J. H. Freese (Cambridge, Mass.: Harvard University Press, 1939), 211.

[34]C. S. Lewis, *They Asked for a Paper* (London: Geoffrey Bles, 1962), 205.

[35]Schneider, 14, 15.

[36]Peter Marin, "The New Narcissism," *Harpers,* Oct. 1975, 17.

[37]Schneider, xviii.

[38]H. M. Lynd, *On Shame and the Search for Identity* (New York: Harcourt, Brace & Co., 1958), 29. Lynd draws heavily on the concept and usage of shame in Western literature, especially in several key figures such as Philip in *Of Human Bondage* by W. Somerset Maugham, Kitty in *Anna Karenina* by Leo Tolstoy, Dimitri Karamazov in *The Brothers Karamazov* by Fyodor Dostoyevsky, and Kafka's *The Trial.*

[39]Thomas Burgess, *The Physiology or Mechanism of Blushing* (London: John Churchill, 1939), 156; cited by

Schneider, *Shame,* 2. Interestingly, Darwin took an interest in the phenomenon of blushing and wrote of it in the last chapter of his *The Expression of the Emotions in Man and Animals.* Darwin saw blushing as "the most peculiar and most human of all expressions," and interestingly, for all his evolutionary thought, doubted that any animal could blush. The relation of humanness to blushing is also seen in the arguments about whether Negroes and Indians blushed. As one commentator put it: "Establishing that the dark-skinned race do indeed blush was not just a foolishness or pedantry since it was involved in a sense of their full humanity."

[40]Kurt Riezler, *Man, Mutable and Immutable* (New York: Regenery, 1951), 202.

[41]Lynd, 20.

[42]Jean-Paul Sartre, *Being and Nothingness* (New York: Philosophical Library, 1956), 222, 259, 260.

[43]Ibid., 221, 222.

[44]Schneider, 25.

10 You Can't Fire Me: I Quit!

"I do not want my name mentioned before the church except to tell them that I withdraw my membership immediately. . . ." So declared Marian Guinn in her letter on September 24, 1981, a few days before the church read its letter to the congregation on October 4, taking disciplinary action against Marian and withdrawing fellowship from her.

And precisely here is what has made the *Guinn* case troublesome. Many observers have sincerely queried whether or not it was any longer the church's business once she quit. What is the point, after all, of disciplining someone who has already withdrawn? Isn't it adding insult to injury and an unnecessary act? Why fire someone who has quit?

Indeed, the attorney for Marian in an early brief opposing the defendant church's motion for dismissal of the lawsuit argued:

Plaintiff admits that within the context of church discipline, it may be possible for those in authority to carry on sufficient conversation to discipline the members according to the rules of the organization. However, plaintiff submits to the court that she was entitled to cease to associate with the organization; that she did so cease; and that any right which the members of said organization had to gossip about her and make known matters of her private life was thereby lost. . . . Any subsequent publication of private matters regarding [Marian Guinn] after the withdrawal were not privileged and were subject to action for invasion of privacy.[1]

In fact, the *Guinn* case's key legal issue on appeal may well be the legal relevance of her resignation. The court might not question the right of churches to practice church discipline among members but will still have to decide whether or not the resignation of a member bars the church from any disciplinary action. In other words, are the rights the church normally has as an association or as a religious body lost when a member resigns? This is the argument in *Guinn:* that whatever rights and legal privileges the Church of Christ had to talk about Marian's private affairs were lost when she quit. This is not a minor issue, because if resignation stops discipline, the practical effect may substantially interfere with church discipline as it has been historically practiced. Should that be the law? Will the Oklahoma Supreme Court buy that? *Does withdrawal silence all comment?*

While our purpose in this volume is not primarily to argue the *Guinn* case, it does provide a framework for reviewing these issues, and in connection with the questions of the relevance of resignation the *Guinn* case is instructive.

First, note that this is not a case where a person resigned a substantial period prior to any church discipline. In fact, the resignation occurred just days before the final steps and long after the initial disciplinary processes were already under way. In many ways it

THE RELEVANCE OF RESIGNATION

seems as if it were a move deliberately intended to preempt any pending discipline. This was not a person without a present and ongoing relationship to the church and its leadership. Rather, as the facts well demonstrate, Marian had been an active member of the church, and even in recent times the relationship was persistent. Marian's resignation was not simply the recognition or formalization of a non-relationship.

Where the resignation occurs long before any contemplated church disciplinary action the relationship may, in fact, have become so negligible and tenuous that statements in the church regarding the person's life are no longer of any legitimate interest to the members. The members may be curious, even snoopy, but there is no continuing relationship or present impact from the relationship that makes that interest legitimate or that makes the information necessary to the church and its members. Courts in such cases might find an invasion of privacy, a sort of intrusive meddling. But that is hardly the case in *Guinn* or in most church discipline situations.

We do not believe resignation is legally or pastorally irrelevant, but the appropriateness of sharing information within the church body ought to rest on factors other than mere formal membership. The issue of whether or not there is a legitimate present interest and relevance to the community in the private information surely ought not to turn on the clever timing of a letter of resignation. Otherwise we could have all kinds of legal questions: What if the resignation has been mailed but not yet received? What if it is communicated to an agent? What about a lost telegram of resignation? What if the party resigns in the middle of a vote?

Second, as Professor McGoldrick noted, the

judge in *Guinn* seemed to give special significance to the resignation as if it were a key element in assessing liability, and yet neither he nor the jury limited damages to events after the resignation. If Marian's resignation were the decisive point after which the privilege to disclose private facts was lost, then presumably damages would be appropriate only for invasions of privacy or other wrongful acts after the resignation—but no such limits were imposed on the jury. The question of the resignation was a largely misunderstood and misapplied issue.

LEGAL ASPECTS

First of all, it is clear as a matter of law that Marian had the right to withdraw her formal membership, and the withdrawal of membership was effective immediately upon notice to the church. Obviously no one may be compelled to belong to a voluntary association. The judge in *Guinn* so instructed the jury:

You are instructed under the law, the plaintiff had the right to terminate her membership with the church upon communication of that fact to an authorized representative of the church at any time.

This instruction is consistent with the law of associations that provides for such unilateral resignation[2] effective immediately without any action by the association required.[3] While an organization may set forth procedures governing the manner of resignation or withdrawal,[4] attempts by associations to create bylaws that provide that associations may deny or reject attempted resignations either by affirmative rejection or refusal to act on a letter of resignation have been held invalid on the grounds they are unreasonable and arbitrary.[5] But how does a termination affect the church's legal rights, both religious and associational, to carry out internal disciplinary and educative processes? Marian may well quit and, if necessary, obtain legal relief and force the church to remove her name from the membership roll. The mere fact that Marian may quit ought not, however, totally bar the church from carrying out its own processes of removing persons from its spiritual community. While the church cannot stop Marian from quitting, she should not be able to bar the church from completing its theologically based processes for terminating the relationship. This seems especially clear in cases such as *Guinn* where she voluntarily joined a church with a theology and practice that included specific convictions about membership. She ought not to be able to complain about the processes of dealing with members of an organization she voluntarily joined that publicly held such views. Legally, it would seem she has waived a right to complain of such practices since she submitted herself to them.

Furthermore, in the case of *Guinn* and perhaps many others the actual conduct subject to disclosure took place during a period of membership not subsequent to resignation. While not conclusive, this supports a legitimate interest in such information and weakens the argument that the resignation somehow bars any disclosure.

It is critical to recognize the continuing legal right of any association, and especially a religious community, to carry out its internal discipline and education of remaining members even after one has resigned.

To hold that the resignation bars further action or comment by an association regarding its relationship to the resigned member could produce bizarre results. Would not the Pope be surprised to learn that after Henry VIII resigned from the church he was barred from commenting on or excommunicating

Henry for his adulterous affair? Would it not seem strange to contend that the California Bar Association was barred from taking further disciplinary action or expressing its views on Nixon's conduct merely because he resigned from the Bar before they issued statements or took formal action?

Should the Boy Scouts be precluded from advising parents regarding a troop leader who had been caught in immoral conduct merely because, having been found out, the scout leader resigned a few hours before the scheduled parents' meeting?

These hypothetical situations illustrate the fact that notwithstanding a resignation, there may continue to be a legitimate community of interest in the information—an interest that derives from the associational relationship and that is not totally and immediately extinguished by the resignation.

We believe the law ought to recognize a continuing right of an association to engage in certain disciplinary acts including the communication of some private facts. This right arises from the independent legitimate interests of the remaining members and because in certain circumstances the group's relationship with the resigned member is such that there is a continued legitimate interest in the community in regard to that person's conduct.

If the courts apply a test other than formal membership, what should it be? The key is whether there is a legitimate interest that sustains the privilege to share private facts in spite of the resignation; it could be called "wrapping up" the membership relationship. In determining whether or not there is a legitimate interest there is a more functional test than formal membership. One must assess whether the body from which the party resigned has a continuing legitimate interest that negates any claim of improper invasion of privacy or invalid exercise of associational discipline. At least the following factors should be considered: (1) the nature of the present relationship between the person and the church, including any resignation and its timing, and the prior nature of relationships that impact the present; (2) the nature of the conduct that was the occasion of the discipline and its *present* impact on the organization and its members; (3) when the supposed private facts (usually conduct) took place relative to the time of membership and resignation—that is, whether the conduct occurred during the period where there was a clear privilege based on membership; (4) the necessity, for purposes of the internal affairs of the church, for church members to be informed of certain otherwise private facts; and (5) the actual or reasonable expectations regarding church disciplinary practices created by church doctrine and practice and the extent of the disciplined person's implied or actual acceptance of those beliefs and practices by virtue of his or her membership.

Applying such a test (including the factors suggested) to a case like *Guinn*, it is apparent that the community interest remains legitimate.

An additional factor to be weighed, discussed in a later chapter, is the constitutional warning against state inhibition of the free exercise of religion and the dangers of theological entanglement when the courts interfere in the internal affairs of churches, including disciplinary processes.

THEO-LOGICALLY SPEAKING

We have noted the clear rule regarding an individual's legal right to withdraw membership from an association or church. The church, of course, may view membership dif-

ferently from a theological perspective. A
church is not like the Rotary Club but a family where relationships are not severed by
one-sided announcements. The Collinsville
church, from a theological perspective, took
the position that membership could not be
unilaterally terminated but that the church
would have to take formal action to sever
ties, which it subsequently did in "withdrawing fellowship."

We must not, however, confuse the legal
question of formal membership with the issue of "withdrawing fellowship," which is
an ecclesiastical and theological decision. We
maintain that as a matter of both theology
and law, the resignation does not destroy
completely the relationship nor the independent rights of the association to assess its
own response to the resignation, including
other sanctions that the association may
properly take.

Part of the confusion here rests with theological misunderstandings held by courts
and even many believers. First, we need to
recognize that both the biblical and the general associational bases for discipline are not
exclusively oriented toward the disciplined
party. What the Collinsville church was doing, and what church discipline is all about,
is not simply a process of expelling unwanted members. If that were all that was involved then a quiet resignation would indeed
be adequate and further action could be
called sheer spite. But this is not the issue.
The disciplined person is not the key actor or
focus. In fact, the person under discipline often is absent from direct contact with the
church. What is said to the congregation or
elders is not chiefly for the individual who
leaves but for those who remain.

Discipline has multiple dimensions. Of
course, an important aspect is to encourage

the sinner to face the consequences of his
conduct and invite repentance and restoration. But it also serves other purposes: (1) it
advises the members of what has happened
within their community in which they have a
continuing spiritual and communal investment; (2) it identifies the responsibilities and
duties of the members toward the disciplined person—such as praying for the other
person, continuing to encourage him to
amend his conduct, or perhaps avoiding certain dealings with him; (3) the publication of
the action serves also as a warning to the remaining members of the moral or theological
commitments of the community and the consequences of rejecting those values and commitments. These are some of the critical
aspects of church discipline that go beyond
the formalities of dismissal and expulsion.

A valuable aspect of church discipline, and
one prominent in the Collinsville church,
deals with instructions to the remaining
members on what their attitude and response is to be toward the one who has left.
Discipline serves an educative function within the remaining community. This purpose is
valid whether or not the person has already
withdrawn. As part of this, the church leadership or congregation may need to be informed of the actions that have been taken
by all parties, the spiritual and religious implications of those, and the spiritual duties
that they continue to have toward one another and toward the one who has left. In
the case of a resignation, a legal dismissal
from membership is obviously no longer necessary, but the church may, according to its
own internal theology and practices, need to
take formal action in regard to membership.

Further, from a biblical and theological perspective, membership in a legal sense is not
the key to a spiritual relationship. Only a

mechanistic theology would take the position that such withdrawal severs all relationships, terminating responsibility and ministry. In fact, any religious community would probably recognize that to some extent spiritual relationships do not exist solely on the basis of legal memberships. When one has been a part of a community for years, where one has been nurtured by and cared for others, a letter of resignation does not sever the personal relationships that exist. This ongoing, albeit changed, relationship may require the church to instruct its members on their spiritual duties toward a former member. This is what the Collinsville church did, and those pronouncements prompted Marian Guinn's lawsuit. In fact, a resignation under circumstances similar to Marian's may require special clarification to the members so that they do not misunderstand the character of the relationship that now ought to exist among them.

The key fact, as we have emphasized, is the nature of the relationship, not the status of formal membership. There might even be a situation in which a person who is not and never has been a formal member might be subject to church discipline. Where one has by virtue of presence and involvement created a relationship with a church it may be appropriate and necessary to exercise a limited form of church discipline in regard to that person's conduct. Suppose a frequent and active (but nonmember) attender at a church is known to be involved in immoral business dealings or involved in an ongoing affair with one of the members. In such cases and other similar scenarios it would seem quite proper for the church to advise its members regarding their relationship to such a person and its moral judgments about the situation. Here again the action would not be to dismiss the offender, since there is no membership, but to advise the church about certain conduct and its implications for the offender's relationship to the church and the members. To use legal language, the person's continued presence would have subjected him or her to the jurisdiction of church discipline.

PRACTICAL PROBLEMS

The effect of holding that a resignation bars any further disciplinary proceedings is strange; it would give the offending member virtual veto power over any comment of the church regarding his or her conduct. As the moment of potentially embarrassing revelation is about to occur, the process is suddenly stopped and all parties silenced by the announcement, "I quit!"

Of course, churches in a given case may decide not to proceed with any formal church disciplinary action or issue any statements within the church when a person resigns. Churches may weigh the factors and decide that under all the circumstances any formal discipline is unnecessary. Alternatively, they may decide that the resignation alters the necessary action to be taken and confine it to announcing the resignation and noting that church disciplinary action had been suspended in light of the resignation. In any case, churches are likely to find the scope of church discipline proceedings and the information revealed in them may be less where the person has resigned. However, for the theological reasons already noted, churches may be reluctant to abandon the process entirely. Even where the membership is terminated voluntarily and where it is about to be terminated by the church for just cause, there may be a spiritual duty to advise other related parties. In the *Guinn* case, the parties were sister churches with whom the Collinsville church had an ongoing relationship and with whom they shared reciprocal duties in regard to persons who might seek membership or relationship with them.

A final note is of critical significance. Should the higher appeal courts of Oklahoma sustain the apparent legal theory of the trial court that Marian Guinn's resignation served to silence the church, it will reflect a tragic misperception of the nature and purpose of the church. Such a conclusion represents a severe interference with the internal affairs of the church, and its effect will be to bind and silence the church in its moral and educative function; or it could force the church and its leaders to risk their institutional and personal property to be faithful to a biblical mandate. It will compel persons to choose between following what they perceive as a command of Scripture and submitting to the power of the state.

NOTES

[1]*Guinn v. Church of Christ of Collinsville*, No. 81-929 (Dist. Ct. Tulsa County, Okla., filed Nov. 23, 1981).

[2]See, for example, *Church of God of Decatur v. Finney*, 101 N.E.2d 856 (Ill. App. 1951); *Fuchs v. Meisel*, 60 N.W. 773 (Mich. 1894); *Trustees of Pencader Presbyterian Church v. Gibson*, 22 A.2d 782 (Del. 1941); *Katz v. Singerman*, 127 So. 2d 515 (La. 1961). In *Gibson* the court stated: "It is incontestable so far as the individual defendants are concerned. Their right, individually or collectively, to withdraw themselves from the Parent Church is protected to the fullest extent by the Constitution of this State." In *Brady v. Reiner*, 198 S.E.2d 812 (W. Va. App. 1973), the court stated, "The Civil Courts freely recognize and affirm the right of any individual or group to leave, abandon or separate from membership in a church." There is an interesting decision in one court that held that a resignation from a professional society where the person was under charges at the time

was not effective. *Ewald v. Medical Society*, 144 App. Div. 82, 128 N.Y.S. 886 (1911).

[3]*People* ex rel. *Haas v. New York Motor Club*, 70 Misc. 603, 129 N.Y.S. 365 (1911).

[4]See *Colonial Country Club v. Richmond*, 19 La. App. 272, 140 So. 86 (1932); *Ewald v. Medical Society*, 144 App. Div. 82, 128 N.Y.S. 886 (1911); *Boston Club v. Potter*, 212 Mass., 23, 98 N.E. 614 (1912).

[5]*Haynes v. Annandale Golf Club*, 4 Cal. 2d 28, 47 P.2d 470 (1935). See also Annot., 99 A.L.R. 1441 (1935).

11 SCALING THE WALL: CONSTITUTIONAL DEFENSES

Congress shall make no law respecting an establishment of religion or prohibiting the free exercise thereof.
First Amendment, *United States Constitution*

"None of the church's business," was Marian Guinn's characterization of her conduct. Many others agreed it wasn't everybody's business and particularly that the discipline of the Collinsville church was "none of the court's business."

Matters of church discipline are wholly outside the purview of secular courts and civil judgments, insist many church leaders and legal scholars. Here, perhaps, is the seminal issue not only in *Guinn* but in the larger arena as well. Is the court, in effect, tampering with church doctrine? Is it, through the threat of civil penalties, compelling the church to adopt a secular model of privacy and morality? to adjust its practices to a socially acceptable paradigm of the church? Is this really an issue of religious liberty?

Certainly the technical defenses to tort actions for invasions of privacy and infliction of emotional distress are highly relevant and must be asserted by those who defend the church and its leaders. But just as clearly, what is going on in these church discipline cases is more fundamental. There is a deep perception that the real issue is a totally improper governmental intrusion into the internal affairs of the church, an assault on its moral witness, an interference with its biblically mandated vision and doctrine of the nature of the church. In short, it is a meddling in the affairs of religion that the founders of our country sought to prohibit by the First Amendment's protections against the establishment of religion and the preservation of the free exercise of religion.

The scope of these protections are perennial and fundamental questions of public policy. What is to be the relationship between the life of religious communities and the potentially coercive power of government? These were the questions with which our founders struggled and to which they addressed themselves, however vaguely, in the First Amendment's religion clause: "Congress shall make no law respecting an establishment of religion or prohibiting the free exercise thereof."

Claims rooted in the First Amendment are prominent issues in church discipline cases. While careful litigators will note that under traditional tort defenses and associational rights the actions against the churches ought to be dismissed, the protections for religious liberty most effectively bar this kind of control or punishment.[1]

We believe that for courts to step into the internal counsels of the church, to affect (through threatened civil financial penalties) its preaching and moral proclamation and instruction to its members under facts such as in these cases, is a serious breach of the wall of separation that the court has erected, in part, for the protection of the church.

It is a violation of the proper and constitutionally recognized autonomy of the church in doctrinal and internal affairs and is an invitation to further intrusions by disgruntled dissenters who will seek to use civil legal process to "act out" their criticisms and anger against religious communities.

This conclusion does not require agreement with, much less endorsement of, the particular actions taken by any specific church. Religious liberty claims are not grounded in assent or praise. Religiously based conduct surely includes acts of enormous nobility and courage but also of substantial foolishness and ignorance. Unless we are prepared to defend both kinds, we will have reduced religious liberty to a privilege of those who enjoy momentary majorities—a class that historically offers little promise of moral integrity or quality.

HISTORICAL INTENT

The founders of the nation and drafters of the Constitution had a special commitment to the protection of religious expression, especially from intrusion by the federal or national government.[2] At the center of their concerns was the "core ideal of religious autonomy."[3]

The founders in no way intended to totally expunge religious influence from society since the framers of the First Amendment were from states that provided many legal benefits to religion and legal penalties for irreligion. Five states actually maintained official state churches, and many states had religious requirements for voting. Former Harvard law professor Mark DeWolf Howe insisted that reading the Constitution as a charter for a secular state is to "distort history" and "dishonor the arts of the historian."[4] Justice Story made the same point about the essential religious commitments of the founders when he declared:

Probably at the time of the Constitution . . . the general, if not the universal sentiment in America was that Christianity ought to receive official encouragement from the State. . . . An attempt to level all religions, and to make it a matter of state policy to hold all in utter indifference, would have created universal disapproval if not universal indignation.[5]

Despite such religious commitments, it is also clear that the founders intended some degree of separateness or distinctive spheres for church and state. While the phrases "separation of church and state" and "wall of separation" are not part of the Constitution (and have been read by some to require a dangerous airtight separation between religion and society), the images of a "wall" do reflect a commitment to avoid improper intrusions into each other's spheres. In fact, long before Thomas Jefferson used the "wall of separation" image in a letter to the Danbury Baptists (which became the source for later Supreme Court use of that language),[6] Roger Williams had used a similar image but with a different connotation. For Williams there was indeed to be a "wall" but its purpose was not so much to keep the church out of the state where its moral influence was critical but to keep the wilderness of the state from polluting the garden of the church.

. . . when they have opened a gap in the hedge or wall of separation between the garden of the church and wilderness of the world, God hath ever broke down the wall itself, removed the candlestick, and made His garden a wilderness, as at this day. And that therefore, if He please to restore His garden and paradise again, it must of necessity be walled in peculiarly unto Himself from the world . . . [7]

URGENCY OF ISSUES

It is not our purpose here to review the arguments regarding the scope or abuse of the religion clauses under current Supreme Court interpretation. Those issues are lively and the Court's expansive "church-state" load in recent years is a sign of the tensions that now exist between religion and government regulation and a witness to the inadequacy and uncertainty of the Court's legal principles in this area.[8]

It is clear that the legal issues of church discipline are part of a larger, more fundamental issue of government intrusion into religion. Secular regulation of religious activities is a "hot" issue, and litigation and legislation in this field is clearly increasing.[9] Both federal and state governments have regulated this area, including civil rights law, labor law, state licensing, land use, health and safety regulation, and taxing issues. In almost all these cases, issues of the proper role of government and religion have arisen. When is "regulation" improper? When is it breaching the wall? Conversely, when would failure to regulate provide an improper deference to religion—a favoritism that might invoke other establishment clause issues? an exemption that might even be dangerous to society?

Many of these legal issues have raised the question of the scope or importance of what is sometimes called "church autonomy": the right of churches and religious organizations to manage their affairs free of government interference. Drawn more narrowly, the

question is the right afforded by the First
Amendment for church practices involving
church discipline that are rooted in religious
and biblical tradition and church history. Perhaps few instances reflect the troublesome
intrusion into internal doctrinal and membership affairs as do these church discipline
cases.

What protections are afforded by the Constitution and the First Amendment? Can we
find in these principles and in their subsequent Court development a basis for preserving the rights of churches to discipline
their common lives in accord with biblical
mandates? We believe so!

THE RELIGION CLAUSES

While the religion clause in the Constitution is one statement and phrase, it has frequently been noted that it contains two
diverse principles referred to as the "establishment clause" and the "free exercise"
clause. Both reflect limits on the interference
of government with matters of religion. Both
provide protections for religious liberty, and
both are relevant to our inquiry here. One
court declared that both clauses have "the
identical purpose of maintaining a separation
between church and state."[10] While it is an
oversimplification, it has been suggested
that the two clauses may be distinguished
by recognizing that the establishment clause
primarily deals with permissible and impermissible government *benefits,* while the free
exercise clause focuses primarily on permissible and impermissible *burdens* on religion
by government.

Debate is persistent on the relationship between these clauses, and nowhere are these
arguments more evident than in the area of
government regulation of religion. On one
hand it may be argued that such regulation

impinges on the free exercise of religion; on the other hand that it creates an impermissible entanglement of the state with religion in violation of the establishment clause protections.

We will now examine the specific holdings of the Supreme Court on these issues, and discuss how its precedents and analysis might address the issues presented by *Guinn* and other similar cases.

THE AUTONOMY PRECEDENTS: CHURCH PROPERTY CASES

The notion of "separation of church and state" developed before modern church-state jurisprudence and recent cases outlining the analytical tools of "establishment" and "free exercise." Though these terms and concepts were not carefully delineated in the early church property cases, the refusal of the courts to intervene in church affairs was grounded generally in the First Amendment; the principles in these early cases were founded on the same ideas that were later framed by the Court more specifically as "entanglement" or free exercise concerns.[11] The key issue in these early church property cases was the problem of churches or factions of churches asking the Court to decide theological issues. The Court very early expressed its conclusion that it was incompetent to decide issues of doctrine.

In 1871 the Court decided a seminal case involving judicial decisions about church affairs.[12] A faction of the Walnut Street Presbyterian Church of Louisville, Kentucky, had split over disputes regarding slavery and the Civil War. The local congregation, desiring to retain the property, argued that the parent denomination had departed from the doctrine of the church. Hence, they reasoned, the local church was the "true" church, the church that had remained theologically true to the church's historic faith and was, therefore, entitled to the property. The Kentucky Supreme Court agreed and held that while there was a "trust" in which the property was held for the parent church denomination, the "departure from doctrine" by the parent dissolved the trust and the local Kentuckians could have title to the property.

The U.S. Supreme Court reversed and in *Watson v. Jones* declared the Court's theological incompetence:

The law knows no heresy, and is committed to the support of no dogma, the establishment of no sect. . . . All who united themselves to such a body [church/denomination] . . . do so with the implied consent to its government, and are bound to submit to it. But it would be a vain consent and would lead to the total subversion of such religious bodies, if anyone aggrieved by one of their decisions could appeal to the secular courts and have those decisions reversed. It is of the essence of these religious unions, and of their right to establish tribunals for the decision of questions arising among themselves, that those decisions should be binding in all cases of ecclesiastical cognizance, subject only to such appeals as the organization itself provides for.[13]

Watson v. Jones established a principle of deference to hierarchical church decisions, a principle that requires civil courts to accept as final and binding the decisions of church authorities in questions of "discipline, faith, ecclesiastical rule, custom or law."[14] This sweeping deference and the list of forbidden territories seem quite applicable to the discipline, faith, custom, and law of the church in Collinsville!

The *Watson* Court seemingly grounded this decision in several principles that remain persuasive and have immediate relevance for church discipline cases today. First, the

Court spoke of "implied consent," the notion that the parties had by a sort of contract agreed to such a governance: "all who unite themselves to such a body do so with an implied consent to this government, and are bound to submit to it." This principle places an emphasis on the intent or agreement of the parties and relies on broad associational law concepts. It argues that the Court should not change the rules of church life in the middle of the ball game, and that when persons voluntarily join such a group they give their consent to the rules that govern that association.

This principle has been reiterated in subsequent cases. The Court's "implied consent" and "bound to submit" declarations were cited in later Supreme Court cases.[15] Justice Brandeis in *Gonzalez v. Archbishop*[16] applied the contract principle in suggesting that "the decision of the proper church tribunals on matters purely ecclesiastical, although affecting civil rights, are accepted in litigation before the secular courts as conclusive, because the parties in interest made them so by contract or otherwise."

Second, the *Watson* decision was rooted in the conviction of the impermissibility of any court adjudication of doctrinal matters: "the law knows no heresy, and is committed to the support of no dogma, the establishment of no sect." This grounds the deference not so much in agreements among persons as in a larger principle of judicial deference based on the subject matter: religious doctrines. Two factors may be at work in this "hands-off" policy. One is a sense of basic incompetence to deal with such theological questions. Part of the problem is surely one of adequate competence in weighing even organizational issues and rules in the context of religious organizations. One commentator referred to this as the "dismal swamp" problem—the inevitable confusion and disorientation when the courts try to understand and decide issues that involve a vocabulary, logic, and history about which they know nothing.[17] A second factor is the recognition of the highly intrusive character of any theological inquiry and decision making—the sort of engagement with religion that would be later denounced as "excessive entanglement."

Inquiry into religious doctrinal matters has long been held impermissible, and the Court has consistently refused such analysis:

> The religious views espoused by respondents might seem incredible, if not preposterous, to most people. But if those doctrines are subject to trial before a jury charged with finding their truth or falsity, the same can be done with the religious beliefs of any sect. When the triers of fact undertake that task, they enter a forbidden domain.[18]

The deference exists notwithstanding the fact that, as Justice Jackson noted, "The price of freedom of religion or of speech or of the press is that we must put up with, and even pay for, a good deal of rubbish."[19]

The third factor in *Watson*'s avoidance of intermeddling with the church issues reflects a broader type of "jurisdictional" approach that one commentator called "strict deference" in which the Court simply assumes "there is some overriding concern for religious autonomy."[20] The Court noted that examining the validity of ecclesiastical decrees "would deprive these bodies of the right of construing their own church laws, would, . . . in effect, transfer to the civil courts . . . the decision of all ecclesiastical questions."

These principles of deference to the theological and doctrinal affairs of churches have been reiterated and even expanded. In 1952 the Court affirmed a "hands-off" approach to any consideration of church doctrine and internal administrative affairs. Its decision contained constitutional dimensions rooted in the free exercise clause when in *Kedroff v. St. Nicholas Cathedral* the Court struck down a New York law aimed at freeing the American Russian Orthodox Church's St. Nicholas Cathedral from Moscow's control.[21] The issue before the Supreme Court was the validity of a New York statute that had in effect given control to an American-based hierarchy free of Moscow. The Court held the act improper and, citing *Watson,* said that since the matter was really one of religious doctrine, it was "strictly a matter for ecclesiastical government," and any intrusion such as the legislature's was improper. It might at first blush have seemed a simple property issue warranting the Court's involvement. But, as the Court noted, "St. Nicholas Cathedral is not just a piece of real estate. . . . What is at stake here is the power to exert religious authority."[22]

The Court spoke of a "spirit of freedom for religious organizations, power to decide for themselves, free from state interference, matters of church government as well as those of faith and doctrine."[23]

Harvard law professor Laurence Tribe, in commenting on this case, notes the importance of the Court's recognition of the doctrinal character of the real issue even when the surface questions may seem legally justifiable and the dangers of permitting dissidents to have a "judicial platform" from which to air their "religious differences with others and potentially win a favorable verdict." He warns of the dangers of permitting an "open season on churches." Tribe concludes:

It is not only the sanctity of religious conscience in the abstract that has been of concern in these cases; it has also been the integrity of religious associations viewed as organic units. . . . Thus, the Supreme Court has recognized for nearly a quarter century that, whatever may be true of other private associations, religious organizations as spiritual bodies have rights that require distinct organizational protection.[24]

The *Watson* principles seem directly relevant to *Guinn* and its successors. The recognition of "implied consent" of persons who voluntarily join the church, the dangers of intrusion into church doctrine even when on the surface the issues may appear to be purely secular, such as tort issues, and the "strict deference" concepts all would argue against any court jurisdiction in these matters. Here the Oklahoma court chose to enter the "dismal swamp," and it has become lost, out of its element. Lacking adequate appreciation of this new arena, it has chartered its own course based on purely secular imagery and direction. No wonder it is disoriented.

The same strict deference seemed to be at work in a case with marked similarities involving leadership struggles in the Serbian Orthodox Church.[25] Milivojevich had been suspended and defrocked in 1963 by the mother church of the Serbian Orthodox Church in Belgrade. The Illinois Supreme Court ordered the bishop's reinstatement, contending that the prescribed church procedure was not followed and that the actions of the mother church had been arbitrary, thus justifying judicial interference and setting aside the official hierarchy's decision. The U.S. Supreme Court held, however, that the Illinois Court had engaged in an "impermissible rejection of the decisions" of the church and that this type of detailed review exceeded the scope of civil court inquiry into ecclesiastical affairs. To allow a review of the criteria by which a church made its decisions is "exactly the inquiry that the First Amendment prohibits." The Court extended protections from review to "disputes over church polity and church administration" and set a high wall when it declared

[it is] the essence of religious faith that ecclesiastical decisions are reached and are to be accepted as matters of faith whether or not rational or measurable by objective criteria. Constitutional concepts of due process, involving secular notions of "fundamental fairness" or impermissible objectives, are therefore hardly relevant. . . .[26]

Presbyterian Church in the U.S. v. Mary Elizabeth Blue Hull Memorial Church was a dispute involving two Georgia Presbyterian congregations that sought to withdraw from the Presbyterian Church in the U.S. alleging doctrinal departure. The U.S. Supreme Court reversed a Georgia court and the jury findings, reiterating that the First Amendment barred the courts from interpreting and weighing doctrines, though it could utilize "neutral principles of law" in property disputes. The Court said again that civil courts "must defer to the resolution of issues of religious doctrine or polity to the highest court of a hierarchical church organization."[27]

These decisions reflect a broad principle of deference to churches in their internal discipline and life, a deference that is rooted in a recognition that courts are improper forums for such debate and represent dangerous threats to the integrity of religious life and organizations. Such principles seem especially relevant in the context of church discipline cases.

These deference principles grounded generally in the First Amendment are reinforced by the Court's more specific explications of the scope of the establishment and free exercise clauses.

As surprising as it is to many, the Supreme Court did not base a decision on, or explain, the establishment clause until 1947 in *Everson v. Board of Education. Everson* questioned whether or not the use of state tax money to reimburse parents for the cost of transporting their children to parochial schools was a violation of the constitutional prohibition against an "establishment of religion."[28]

ESTABLISH- MENT CLAUSE

It was this case that established the so-called "separationist" tradition of the court. Justice Hugo Black, writing for the Court, drew heavily on Jefferson's letter to the Danbury Baptists and declared the First Amendment erected a "wall of separation between church and state" that must be "high and impregnable" so that not even the "slightest breach" could be approved. A year later in *McCollum v. Maryland*, Justice Felix Frankfurter in a concurring opinion affirmed this separationist faith: "We renew our conviction that we have staked the very existence of our country on the faith that complete separation of church and state is best for the state and for religion. . . . 'Good fences make good neighbors.'"[29]

Despite popular and academic criticism of the imagery of a "wall of separation," the metaphor stuck and has dominated church-state jurisprudence since that time.[30]

But what is the wall for? What is it keeping out? or in? Over the next several years after *Everson,* in cases primarily dealing with government aid to parochial schools, the Court developed a test for determining whether or not there has been an impermissible "establishment" of religion. Its test is usually referred to as the "tripartite test" because of its three primary types or manifestations of prohibited establishment. In 1977 the Supreme Court in *Wolman v. Walter* summarized the requirements of the establishment clause:

In order to pass muster, the statute must have a clear secular legislative purpose, must have a principal or primary effect that neither advances nor inhibits religion, and must not foster excessive government entanglement with religion.[31]

The magic words thus are *purpose, effect,* and *entanglement.* That is, any government action whose purpose is to aid or inhibit religion rather than being based on a legitimate secular end, or that has the primary effect of aiding or inhibiting religion, or that results in excessive entanglement of government with religion, is constitutionally invalid. These tests—purpose, effect, entanglement—are not terribly precise. They seem to be the ways in which the court *describes* what it does, not the means by which it *determines* it. But they are dominant categories in any legal analysis.

ENTANGLE-MENT

The discrete interests of government and religion are mutually best served when each avoids too close a proximity to the other.[33]

While one might argue that government support for the intrusions illustrated by *Guinn* violates the "purpose" or "effect" prongs of the tripartite test (by arguing, for example, that the effect is to favor certain kinds of churches and penalize those that emphasize a strong disciplined membership,[34] the more promising and relevant element for legal debate is the nonentanglement requirement.[35]

The basic idea of avoiding entanglement is, as we have noted, older than the modern cases that have enunciated it. It reflects a judgment shared by many of the founders and expressed succinctly by Madison. He insisted that the national government "has not a shadow of right . . . to intermeddle with religion."

The nonentanglement principle was first formally announced in *Walz v. Tax Commission* (1970) in which the court upheld a tax exemption for a religious organization noting that the exemption was permissible in part because nontaxation permitted a lower degree of entanglement between government and religion. In *Lemon v. Kurtzman*, the excessive entanglement principle was affirmed and made the third prong of the tripartite test. In *Lemon* this prohibition was violated because the state aid required some state auditing procedures to prevent misuse of aid intended for secular aspects of a private school.

Obviously "excessive" entanglement is prohibited. It is by no means self-evident what is "excessive" since the test lacks clarity and precision.[36] Justice Byron White once referred to the test as "curious and mystifying."

Some entanglement is inevitable. Tax exemption is an entanglement of sorts since it requires some assessment of whether "religion" exists. Providing public services such as highways and sewer connections or providing police protection to churches creates some interweaving of relations. What about judicial protection of church property? Even court mandated and enforced protections against infringements of religious freedom would require some "entangling."[37]

What we must avoid, therefore, are relationships that somehow create "excessive" entanglements. The court has tended to identify several different kinds of impermissible entanglements. First is doctrinal entanglement. We have already noted the deference given to the church on matters of theology; judicial review is in some sense an impermissible "theological" or doctrinal entanglement.

Second is administrative entanglement. The early cases in which entanglement principles were often applied focused on an impermissible administrative entanglement. The Court in *Lemon* spoke of the dangers of "comprehensive, discriminating and continuing"[38] surveillance of the programs, use of funds, and accounting by churches and religious groups whenever federal aid goes to religious schools. Such surveillance involves the government in the kinds of review and monitoring that are anathema to the Constitution. In *Walz* the Court noted that it was critical to avoid contexts where there was any "governmental evaluation" of religious practices, "state investigation into church operations," or any involvement of government in "difficult classifications of what is or is not religious."[39]

Clearly the Court is concerned about excessive government surveillance. The most troublesome form of all surveillance, however, is any governmental attempt to resolve internal religious disputes. Laurence Tribe insists that

the form of entanglement the Supreme Court deems most subversive of First Amendment values is that which involves government not only in the apparatus of religion but in its very spirit—in its decision on core matters of belief and ritual.[40]

While the concept of entanglement initially developed in "aid" cases, it clearly is applicable to "regulation" cases as well. That is, the doctrine developed where the issue was the permissible scope of government aid and when such aid created an excessive entanglement. But increasingly the doctrine is being used where the issue is the permissible scope of government control and whether such control creates precisely the kind of intrusion barred as excessive. It is here that the doctrine argues strongly for court deference to the disciplinary, doctrinal, and instructional aspects of the church's life.

It seems clear that allowing the courts to decide when a person is subject to church discipline, when the members of a church may be advised of disciplinary action taken against a member or former member including the conduct that caused the discipline, and imposing tort liability based on its decision is precisely the kind of *excessive* entanglement that the Supreme Court has sought to avoid.

ENTANGLE-MENT AND CHURCH DISCIPLINE

Lower courts have recognized the dangers of such interference and consistently resisted intrusion into such internal affairs, recognizing that "in matters purely religious or ecclesiastical, the civil courts have no jurisdiction."[41] Or consider the decision of the Nebraska Supreme Court that asserted that religious freedom itself would not long survive if members disgruntled about "some matter of religious faith or church polity could successfully appeal to the secular courts for redress."[42]

In these church discipline cases, the level of court intrusion into the church's life is clear and multiple. It touches basic doctrinal issues including the nature and meaning of membership, the duties imposed by biblical passages such as Matthew 18 in regard to the discipline of members, the sort of conduct that properly results in the discipline of members whether or not they choose to quit before the process is complete, the moral weight given different types of conduct, and the right of a church to develop its own administrative rules and internal organizational structures—that is, its own constitution and bylaws.

It seems clear that court-imposed penalties of the sort ordered in *Guinn* represent tragic entanglements with the life of the church that seriously breach the wall of proper separation. These are not peripheral or incidental aspects of church life—they go to the core of the concerns and character of the religious community. Recall that the legal action was based largely on the content of teaching and preaching done by the elders and pastor to the church in connection with a formal service of the church and a business meeting. For this conduct, the court awarded punitive damages.

FREE EXERCISE AND CHURCH AUTONOMY

A right to church autonomy under the free exercise clause focuses on the real issues at stake. The right is the right of churches to make for themselves the decisions that arise in the course of running their institutions.[43]

Free exercise claims emerge in terms of individuals and also in the context of group or communal interests.[44] Many, perhaps most, religious exercises take place in the context of communities of faith, and free exercise rights ought to include the rights of these communities to carry out their lives of worship, discipline, and management without interference from the government.

The protections of free exercise of religion

are urgent in a society that is becoming increasingly pluralistic and in which government regulation of life at many levels is
growing. Such an environment is often in-
hospitable to the demands and vigor of religious faith. The preservation of an open
forum for religious life is critical not only to
protect the vitality of religion and of individual conscience but also because there are
sound public policy grounds for recognizing
the value of a strong moral and prophetic
voice in society. This voice at times will
speak against the culture, even the government itself. Given the urgent issues in contemporary society—environmental crises,
war and peace, biomedical revolution, human rights—no society ought to diminish the
voice of any moral resources.

Religion must be free to be countercul-
tural, out of step with society.[45] Otherwise
religion is forced to mirror society, to be a
lackey of the spirit of the age. It will be
forced to be thoroughly "worldly." In such a
world, the prophetic and moral witness of religion would be lost.[46]

The totalitarian state, of course, will resist
any alternative center of authority, accountability, and moral suasion. But a government
sensitive to the character of moral life and
the vagaries of human existence, including
the culpability of government itself, will be
eager to assure maximum liberty in the expression of moral thought.

As with the establishment clause, the issue of free exercise was a late-comer to the
Court, but in modern times it has developed
a test by which it analyzes free exercise
claims. In *Cantwell*,[47] *Barnette*,[48] *Sherbert*,[49]
and *Yoder*[50] the Court has developed strong
commitments to free exercise protections
and insisted that, as Justice Burger put it in
Yoder, "It must appear either that the State

does not only deny the free exercise of religious belief by its requirement, or that there is a state interest of sufficient magnitude to override the interest claiming protection under the free exercise clause ... only those interests of the highest order and not otherwise served can overbalance legitimate claims to the free exercise of religion."

These cases have resulted in the following test or process of free exercise analysis: (1) Can the claimant or plaintiff show that a government action has burdened, directly or indirectly, the exercise of a sincerely held religious belief? (2) If so, has the state shown that the burden or infringement is justified or necessary by a compelling state interest? (3) Even if there is a compelling interest, has the state chosen means to achieve those legitimate overriding interests that are the least intrusive on religious liberty?

Therefore, the free exercise clause of the First Amendment requires that substantial burdens on the free exercise of religion must be justified by compelling state interests. As the Supreme Court declared in *Wisconsin v. Yoder,* "Only those interests of the highest order ... can overbalance legitimate claims to the free exercise of religion."

LIMITS

Clearly, under this analysis, not every claim to free exercise will prevail. Courts have noted that there are interests of the state that will overcome the right of free exercise. For example, in an early case the Supreme Court rejected the claim that religious duties requiring polygamy were protected by the free exercise clause.[51] In *Bob Jones University v. United States* the governmental interest in eradicating racial discrimination was found to be sufficient to overwhelm the racially discriminatory practices of the university.[52]

While free exercise of religion encompasses both the freedom to believe and the
freedom to act, these cases illustrate that
the latter is not absolute. One's conduct is
not totally immune from government sanc-
tion merely because one labels it, even accurately, as religiously motivated. Thus, courts
have consistently held that under proper circumstances courts may restrain religious exercises and punish illegal conduct even if in
the furtherance of religion. Obvious examples would be prohibitions against child sacrifice or religious parades down Main Street
at the height of rush hour.

To contend therefore that the government
is exceeding its limits of intrusion under the
facts of present church discipline cases is
not to assert that the church is immune from
public accountability no matter what it does.
There are compelling interests that can overcome the heavy presumption of noninterfer-
ence. Can one imagine a church discipline
situation where the state's interest would
overcome the religious organization's discipline practices? Surely! As Professor McGoldrick has suggested, should a church claim
the right to beat a sinner into repentance or
lock him up until he has a repentant heart,
the state's interest in that individual's safety
would prevail. The church would be subject
to the appropriate criminal penalties and civil remedies.

One can now apply these free exercise protections to the practices of the church in
church discipline cases.

First, does the involvement of the civil
court in rendering judgments against
churches for carrying out these religiously
motivated practices constitute a burden or
infringement?

**FREE
EXERCISE
AND
DISCIPLINE**

All logic would say yes. To demand that church elders and pastors exercise church discipline in keeping with their religious faith and practices only at the risk of catastrophic liability in civil suits utilizing the machinery of the state certainly is a burden on the exercise of religion.

The mere fact that the form of the legal action sounds like a purely secularly grounded claim does not, as we have seen in the church property cases, negate the essentially religious character of the issue. Calling the action a modern tort ought not confuse the courts about the infringement on religious exercise. Few cases impact directly on religion.

Second, is there a compelling state interest that justifies this burden or intrusion? We believe not!

Is this the sort of case that warrants intrusion and control? Is this a case involving such an outrage against the conscience and civilized society that the state must act as the plaintiffs allege? Is there some great societal interest in awarding Marian punitive damages for her church's truthful revelations? Is this interest greater than that of the religious practices of the church? Only a total insensitivity to the value of religious autonomy, the integrity of the church, and the relevance of disciplinary standards could cause one to insist that Marian's alleged right of privacy in her affair is more important. Perhaps only a society that wished to silence such churches because it had little respect for their values would insist that on the societal scale the church interests weigh little compared with Marian's.

The claims based on the dignitary torts in Collinsville do not seem to come even close to outweighing the damage to religious liberty and free exercise.

Surely an aspect of the free exercise right of any religious community is the right to determine its own procedures for admitting new members, canceling membership, and disciplining members. The state would seem to have no legitimate interest in interfering in such doctrinal decisions. The Court's own principles have caused it to give great deference to the church in determining internal organization and doctrinal commitments and practices.

If the court cannot interfere with hierarchical decisions of the church regarding true factions or the disposition of church property, even where the acts of churches may seem arbitrary to outsiders, how can it become a party to deciding doctrines regarding membership procedures?

THE THREAT

But the Court's free exercise analysis does raise potential problems. We believe the test itself is fundamentally sound and necessary. There are limits to free exercise and they are precisely where the Court has put them: when there is a clearly overriding or compelling state interest. But there are two danger points that could effectively strip these apparent protections of religious liberty.

First, since one must show a burden on the exercise of a religious belief before the remainder of the test is applicable, any tendency to shrink the scope of "religion," to narrow its definition, will have the effect of minimizing the protections. The potential problem is the basic question of whether or not the courts do, or even can, really understand religion. For Christians and many others, religion is not simply composed of liturgical and ecclesiastical doctrines and practices. It encompasses life. It certainly includes moral teachings. But for too many secularists, religion is perceived as something much narrower. While they are willing to protect religion vigorously in the more narrow "churchy" sense, they are likely to label as "secular" activities that are deeply grounded in religious faith and life. If this labeling is effective, religious liberty is gone because it has been defined out!

As constitutional lawyer William Ball once warned, there is a danger of attempting to squeeze religion into the peace under the steeple. He later described the problem as one of "comprehension" on the part of secularists regarding religion. He spoke of a "disturbing vacuum in some governmental minds [about] religious experience, conversion and the evolution of doctrinal stand," and of the "devastating judicial misconception of religion which has truly revolutionized our nation."[53] It will be critical to educate the Court about the essential theological and religious aspects of these practices.

For example, if the actions of the church in Collinsville were seen as not sufficiently religious in character but "secular," then the religious freedom defense is unavailable. The church would be limited to a traditional tort defense posture.

In the recent judgment in *Christofferson v. Church of Scientology* the jury awarded $39 million punitive damages to a former adherent.[54] The first question put to the jury was whether or not the "promises" by the Scientologists were "religious" or "wholly secular." The danger is evident—once church practices are defined as secular, the game may be up!

The second threat concerns the second of the steps in the test: whether or not there is a compelling state interest. Again, the concept and language pose no problem. The danger lurks in the ambiguity of the concept of "compelling state interest." It is not a self-defining term. It is more of a conclusion than an analytical tool. A "compelling state interest" is nothing other than what a judge has decided is more important than other interests at stake. Perhaps such ambiguity is inevitable, but the threat is that such "compellingness" is in fact largely a sociologically and politically assessed reality. Such interests are the products and conclusions of a society. As the values of society evolve and are shaped, as they are now, by a strident secularism and a growing state, those ideas will decide what is "compelling." For example, as government regulatory activity increases, as there are increasing licensing, standards, and other types of state involvement, "compelling" will become an evolutionary and slippery category. The very presence of the state in the arena is likely to create an initial "interest" that soon will be discovered to be "compelling."[55] The danger is that free exercise of religion will be swallowed up in a sea of compelling state interests. The zone left for religious liberty will only be those regions in which the state has not yet taken an active interest. Compelling interests are very likely to be colonialistic and imperialistic. The movement is all in one direction, and it poses ominous trends for the vitality of a broadly conceived religious ministry.

CONCLUSION

These great constitutional principles of church autonomy and deference to church affairs, and the more specific prohibitions against excessive entanglement or infringing on free exercise, are sound policies and assure religious liberty against state intrusion. This deference except under the most compelling circumstances is proper, particularly when any intrusion would impose restraints and controls on the internal and doctrinal affairs of religious bodies. Laycock has correctly pointed out that nowhere are such principles more commanding than when they touch the internal affairs of the church and relationships among members who have voluntarily joined.[56]

We began our analysis in this volume by noting the deep roots church discipline issues have in theology, church history, and spiritual values. We noted that the issues were much more than technical legal questions. We then turned to look at the specific legal issues and defenses in regard to questions such as libel, invasion of privacy, and intentional infliction of emotional distress.

But we have now returned to our starting point—noting that even our legal analysis drives us inextricably into religious inquiry. There is simply no way to escape the moral and religious character of the issues when churches exercise discipline in regard to the moral conduct of their members. There is no escaping the fundamental questions when a society through its courts begins to penalize churches for practices rooted in moral perspectives that the society itself found central and enforced in law until recent years. There is no dodging the basic spiritual and philosophical issues when jurors vent their feelings against churches whose doctrines reflect a commitment largely absent from a relativistic and morally rootless culture. The question is still whether or not church discipline is the business of the courts or the business of the church.

NOTES

[1]Indeed, it might prove to be a tragic mistake to rely solely on traditional associational or contract rights in

building a legal and public policy case for governmental abstention in interfering in church discipline cases. While associational rights are significant, they are of a different class or order than the rights protected by the specific language of the First Amendment. Further, associational rights have increasingly been limited by other state interests and have never had the strong protections that have surrounded religious expressions. The courts have recognized a "preferred" status for certain civil liberties such as religious expression. Legislators and courts are much more willing to overwhelm mere associational rights of clubs, fraternal societies, or interest groups as opposed to intruding into the deeply rooted and conscience-grounded convictions and practices that spring from religion and churches.

[2]The language prohibits "Congress" from enacting any law "respecting" an establishment of religion. Its restraints, thus, were initially limited to federal governmental action and probably were intended to bar any religious interference by the national government, even though state laws at the time did "establish" state churches. Later, most state constitutions provided prohibitions against "establishments" and protections for free exercise of religion. The First Amendment's protections were not made applicable to the states, however, until modern times. In 1940, in *Cantwell v. Connecticut,* 310 U.S. 296 (1940), the Court declared that the Fourteenth Amendment "rendered the legislatures of the states as incompetent as Congress" to enact laws violative of the establishment or free exercise clauses. Thus the First Amendment's religious clause protections are now applicable to any "state action," that is, any act of government, federal or state, and any branch or agent thereof.

[3]Laurence Tribe, *American Constitutional Law* (Mineola, New York: Foundation Press, 1978), 812.

[4]Mark D. Howe, *The Garden and the Wilderness: Religion and Government in American Constitutional History* (Chicago: University of Chicago Press, 1965), 31, 34.

[5]Edward Corwin, *American Constitutional History: Essays,* ed. Mason and Garvey (Magnolia, Mass.: Smith, Peter, n.d.), 205, 206.

[6]*Everson v. Board of Education,* 330 U.S. 1 (1947). Referring to Justice Black's analysis of American history in that case, Mark Howe has declared that the "Court dishonored the work of the historian." Michael Malbin spoke of "an incredibly flawed reading of the intent of the authors [of the First Amendment] by the Court"

(Malbin, *Religion and Politics: The Intentions of the Authors of the First Amendment* [Washington, D.C.: American Enterprise Institute, 1978]). And Edwin Corwin noted that "undoubtedly the Court has a right to make history, but it does not have the right to remake it" (Corwin, "The Supreme Court as a National School Board," 14 *Law and Contem. Prob.* 3, 20 [1949]).

[7]Contrastingly, Jefferson saw the wall as chiefly protecting the state. He would have barred, for example, clergy from holding public office, a policy attempted by Tennessee but struck down by the U.S. Supreme Court in *McDaniel v. Paty,* 435 U.S. 618 (1978).

[8]The church must become more aware of the scope and nature of these issues and struggle with them not merely at the case level but at more fundamental jurisprudential levels as well; that is, What is the proper role of the state? of government in God's order for creation? What is the biblical view of liberty and religious liberty? How ought the church respond to governments that exceed their biblical authority or that act unjustly?

[9]See, for example, the discussion in the article by Ripple, "The Entanglement Test of the Religious Clause—A Ten Year Assessment," 27 *U.C.L.A. L. Rev.* 1195 (1980).

[10]*Catholic Bishop v. NLRB,* 559 F.2d 1112, 1131 (7th Cir. 1977).

[11]In *Serbian Eastern Orthodox v. Milivojevich,* 426 U.S. 696 (1976), the Court simply referred to "the First and Fourteenth Amendments" as barring review by the courts of church decisions.

[12]So described by Ellman, "Driven from the Tribunal: Judicial Resolution of Internal Church Disputes," 69 *Cal. L. Rev.* 1378 (1981).

[13]*Watson v. Jones,* 80 U.S. 679 at 728 (1871).

[14]Ibid., 727.

[15]*Watson v. Jones,* 80 U.S. 679 at 729 (1871), cited in *Serbian Eastern Orthodox Diocese v. Milivojevich,* 426 U.S. 696, 711 (1976).

[16]*Gonzalez v. Archbishop,* 280 U.S. 1, 16 (1929).

[17]Chafee, "The Internal Affairs of Associations Not-For-Profit," *Harv. L. Rev.,* 993, 1021 (1930).

[18]*United States v. Ballard,* 322 U.S. 78, 87 (1944).

[19]Ibid.

[20]See Ellman, "Driven from the Tribunal," 69 *Cal. L. Rev.* 1378 (1981).

21*Kedroff v. St. Nicholas Cathedral,* 344 U.S. 94 (1952).

22344 U.S. at 121, 123 (1952) (Frankfurter, J., concurring).

23Ibid., 116.

24Tribe, 876.

25*Serbian Eastern Orthodox Diocese for the U.S. and Canada v. Milivojevich,* 426 U.S. 696 (1976).

26Ibid., 714, 715.

27*Presbyterian Church in the U.S. v. Mary Elizabeth Blue Hull Memorial Church,* 393 U.S. 440, 446 (1969). The Court did note that it would be permissible to use "neutral principles of law, developed for us in all property disputes," but noted such was not what was required in this case. The concept of employing neutral principles was reaffirmed in *Jones v. Wolf,* 443 U.S. 595 (1979). The concept has drawn considerable critical comment.

28*Everson v. Board of Education,* 330 U.S. 1 (1947).

29*McCollum v. Maryland,* 333 U.S. 203, 232 (1948) (Frankfurter, J., concurring).

30"A rule of law should not be drawn from a figure of speech." *McCollum v. Board of Education,* 33 U.S. 203, 247 (1948) (Reed, J., dissenting). The Court has at times described the wall as "blurred, indistinct and variable" (*Lemon v. Kurtzman,* 403 U.S. 602 [1971]) and even insisted that the Constitution does not require separation in "every and all circumstances" (*Zorach v. Clausen,* 343 U.S. 306 [1952]) and that there must be "room to play in the joints" (*Walz v. Tax Commission,* 397 U.S. 664 [1970]).

31*Wolman v. Walter,* 433 U.S. 229, 236 (1977). The test was really set forth first in *Lemon v. Kurtzman* and is thus occasionally referred to as the "Lemon" test.

32Some commentators have been critical of conceiving of government regulation applied to organizations such as churches as posing "establishment" claims under the entanglement clause and insist that the place to root any exceptions to such is in the free exercise clause. Douglas Laycock argued this in "Towards a General Theory of Religion Clauses: The Case of Church Labor Relations and the Right of Church Autonomy," 81 *Cal. L. Rev.* 1373 (1981). Others such as University of Missouri law professor Carl Esbeck insist that free exercise protections only apply to individuals because only they have consciences that can be coerced; all other protections, such as those afforded a church, must be found precisely in the nonentanglement prohibitions of the establishment clause. But many commentators have insisted that it is well established that collectivities have free exercise rights. Further, any confinement of free exercise to individuals would seem to reflect more of a modern preoccupation with individualism than any realistic or historic sense of the character of religion or the development of conscience.

[33]*Roemer v. Maryland Pub. Works Bd.,* 426 U.S. 736, 772 (1976) (Brennan, J., dissenting).

[34]The effect aspect also prohibits government actions that negatively impact selected religions and thus indirectly aid other religions. It may be argued that the *Guinn* decision discriminates in favor of the impersonal, noninvolved religion. As McGoldrick put it, "Old-fashioned religion is out; drive-in religion is in."

[35]The nonentanglement requirement may, as Laurence Tribe suggests, just be another way of looking at the same information as one would analyze when exploring whether there is an impermissible "effect" of inhibiting or aiding religion. That is, Has the conduct of government created a relationship that has an impermissible effect?

[36]The entanglement analysis of the Court has been critically reviewed in a number of articles. See Gianella, "The Bitter and the Sweet of Church–State Entanglement," 1971 *S. Ct. Rev.* 147; Warner, "NLRB Jurisdiction Over Parochial Schools: *Catholic Bishop of Chicago v. NLRB,*" 73 *Nw. L. Rev.* 463 (1978); Gaffney, "Political Divisiveness Along Religious Lines: The Entanglement of the Court in Sloppy History and Bad Public Policy," 24 *St. Louis U.L.J.* 205 (1980).

[37]Some argue that any "entanglement" is contrary to biblical principles. Apart from the practical problems of such a theory as noted, one may question whether or not such a view is biblical. Is not government a legitimate institution? Does not it have a duty to do justice even when that might involve religious bodies? Is government really just for sinners or nonchurches?

[38]*Lemon v. Kurtzman,* 403 U.S. 602, 619 (1971).

[39]See *Walz,* including the concurring opinions of Justices Brennan and Harlan, and commentary on the case by Tribe, 869. A further kind of impermissible entanglement, less relevant in this context, is the concern over *political* entanglement. The court has referred to political divisiveness created by state involvement with religious belief and practice as a "warning signal not to be ignored." *Committee for Public Education v. Nyquist,* 413 U.S. 756, 797, 798 (1973).

[40]Tribe, 870.

[41]*Watson v. Garvin,* 54 Mo. 353, 378 (1873), cited by Tribe, 871.

[42]*Wehmer v. Fokenga,* 57 Neb. 510, 518, 519, 78 N.W. 28, 36, 37 (1899).

[43]Laycock, 1394.

[44]See footnote 32.

[45]Precedents for religious liberty have most always arisen in connection with unpopular and sociologically bizarre groups. Many early Supreme Court decisions involved such unique groups as Jehovah's Witnesses and Seventh Day Adventists. Today free exercise cases most often involve similarly unpopular groups ranging from the Unification Church and the Hare Krishnas to fundamentalists.

[46]The concern about religion being forced to stay in step with government or public policy was voiced by the concurring opinion of Justice Stewart in *Bob Jones University v. United States,* 103 S. Ct. 2017 (1983). He noted the danger of any concept of qualification for tax exemption that requires groups to reflect public policy instead of a view that recognizes society is best served by a wide open, broad public debate in which even ridiculous and offensive notions are permitted in the marketplace of ideas.

[47]*Cantwell v. Connecticut,* 310 U.S. 296 (1940) voided a breach of the peace conviction against Newton Cantwell and his sons. The Court insisted that "the power to regulate must be so exercised as not, in attaining a permissible end, unduly to infringe the protected freedom."

[48]*West Virginia State Board of Education v. Barnette,* 319 U.S. 624 (1943) sustained a claim that a state statute compelling school children to salute the flag was an infringement of the free exercise of religion. The Court stated that "freedoms of speech and of press, assembly and worship may not be infringed on such slender grounds. They are susceptible of restriction only to prevent grave and immediate danger to interests the State may lawfully protect." In effect the Court was applying a free speech analysis to the religious expression.

[49]*Sherbert v. Verner,* 374 U.S. 398 (1963) involved a successful challenge on free exercise grounds of a denial of unemployment benefits to the plaintiff because she refused to accept work on the Sabbath.

[50]*Wisconsin v. Yoder,* 406 U.S. 205 (1972) sustained an objection by Amish on free exercise grounds of convic-

tion for failure to send their children to secondary schools as mandated by state law.

52*Reynolds v. United States,* 98 U.S. 145 (1878). George Reynolds unsuccessfully asserted a free exercise right to violate federal laws prohibiting polygamy because his practices were rooted in religious convictions. The Court noted that Reynolds was free to believe as he wished, a freedom absolutely guaranteed by the First Amendment, but that Congress was "left free to reach actions that were in violation of social duties or subversive of good order." The Court concluded: "Laws are made for the government of actions, and, while they cannot interfere with mere religious belief or opinion, they may with practices." This has frequently been referred to as the "belief-action" distinction. Later cases have recognized that the First Amendment not only protects belief but much action as well.

52*Bob Jones University v. United States,* 103 S. Ct. 2017 (1983).

53"Religious Liberty in 1984: Perils and Promises," *Quarterly,* 5, no. 4 (1984), 4.

54*Christofferson v. Church of Scientology,* No. A7704-05184 (Cir. Ct. Multnomah County, Oreg., filed July 19, 1985).

55An illustration would be in the arena of education where at the founding of the nation education was clearly not a "compelling interest" of the state, and was hardly an interest at all. Most all education was religious, and all was private. Gradually the state became involved and over a century increasingly became the main source of education with "standards" that it now often seeks to impose on all education both public and private. Courts today acknowledge with hardly a blink a "compelling interest" of the state in education. Without judging whether that evolution has been good or not, it illustrates the manner in which, in a relatively short time, an arena totally outside the purview of government can become almost the monopoly of government, swallowing up the interests of others and overwhelming them.

56Laycock, 1403. Suggesting tests for autonomy, Laycock also notes that the case for autonomy is strongest where the matter is internal and the "religious" aspect of the issue is intense and where the threat of regulation would substantially coerce the church or individual by prohibition or incentives to abandon a religious practice (as opposed to state involvement that might only make such activities somewhat more expensive).

12 STAYING OUT OF COURT

Can they sue us? That is the frequent query of the anxious pastor. The answer is almost invariably *yes!* You can be sued for virtually any reason—all it takes is the payment of a filing fee. Now, being successfully sued is another thing. But there is nothing you can do to assure that you won't be sued.

Whatever the outcome of the appeals in *Guinn*, issues of legal liability in church discipline situations are likely to continue for years. Surely the potential of legal conflicts ought to give us second thoughts about our church discipline practices. Even more critically, our biblical commitments and desires to be a genuine healing community ought to drive us to develop principled approaches to church discipline.

The appeal in *Guinn* may produce any number of results. The appeal could be successful and the whole case dismissed, or it could be returned to a lower court for further proceedings. Liability could be upheld, but on narrow grounds, limiting legal exposure. The court might, for example, give special weight to the resignation. The court even might suggest guidelines. Whatever the decision, the losing side will appeal to the U.S. Supreme Court. Regardless of the outcome, one may expect further tests of these concepts since *Guinn* is the first case of substance grounded in claims of invasion of privacy and emotional distress. Therefore, even if the appeals are totally successful for the church, the issue of potential legal liability may be with us for some time.

But the church is not powerless. There are steps it can take to minimize the likelihood of liability thereby discouraging frivolous lawsuits. When these steps do not compromise any biblical principles or theological convictions they are clearly appropriate. As a matter of fact, often they represent just and reasonable policies and biblically mandated postures and church policies. If *Guinn* helps us all think more self-critically about these issues, it will have served us well.

There are several key areas we believe should be assessed and where the church should implement carefully developed policies and practices. These steps will minimize the risk of lawsuits and, when such issues do emerge, will assist courts in understanding the nature of the commitments to church discipline and their legitimacy.

We are presuming the church will also examine carefully the bases supporting any discipline practices. The theology of the church, its concepts of community, and the manner in which it stimulates a community of mutual responsibility are all highly relevant; indeed, they are prerequisites to the more formal steps noted here. Any attempt to buttress the church with legal protections and carefully articulated policies designed to minimize external interference will not serve the kingdom unless accompanied by a more basic commitment to the church as a redemptive and responsible community under the lordship of Christ. Only such a larger view can also put the legal principles noted in this volume into perspective. Church discipline is first and foremost not a legal problem; it is an issue of ministry. Nevertheless, there are some specific matters that may be helpful in the context of establishing policy.

NOTICE

A central issue, not only in law but in the church as well, is whether or not the members are on notice that their church practices church discipline and on what basis, in what form, and with what processes. Is there knowledge and awareness that the church expects membership to entail certain obligations? It is a matter of simple fairness that one should not hold a person to a standard of conduct that he or she didn't bargain for, agree to, or understand. Church discipline should not be a surprise, much less a shock. It ought to be expected and natural.

Such principles are embodied in our nation's criminal laws by the constitutional prohibition against *ex post facto* (retroactive) laws. Each of us has an innate sense that it is unjust to change the rules in the middle of the game. Where there is no knowledge and therefore no "notice," there is a heightened danger of arbitrariness.

In the *Guinn* case, it is instructive to note that the complaint alleged that Miss Guinn had no knowledge that the church practiced such discipline. There is evidence that the church had in fact given notice of its practices to its members and that Miss Guinn had observed church discipline in practice in the Collinsville church. But the complaint illustrates the importance of disclosure. It is similar to a fair trade provision. Church

membership ought not to be *caveat emptor,*
let the "buyer beware," but a fully disclosed
relationship.

This is not merely a legal principle but a
theological one as well. The expectations,
the character of the church and its values,
the meaning of membership, are not questions that ought to emerge for the first time
at a congregational meeting for expulsion of
an erring member, but should be clearly and
repeatedly manifested. Chuck Colson, commenting on the *Guinn* case, noted that the
concept that personal moral conduct is no
business of the church may be an idea "justified by the way we've acted." He insisted:
"We have to admit that the world's view of
us is not far from the mark. Our culture
doesn't think that morality is any of our business because they haven't seen us *make* it
our business." He concluded with a powerful
prophetic judgment: "It will be bad news if
the court should emasculate the church by
holding that it cannot enforce biblical standards on its members; but it will be even
worse news if it turns out that by ignoring
our biblical responsibilities we have done it
to ourselves."[1]

Thus, notice—the transparent expectations about the nature of the church and
membership in it—is more than a judicial invasion of religious autonomy. Its root principle has to do with integrity, consistency, and
openness.

HOW DO YOU GIVE NOTICE? There are several
ways in which this "notice" ought to be
given.

*1. It ought to be clearly enunciated in the
bylaws of the church.* The governing documents of the church, its constitution and bylaws, ought to express the basic convictions
about the nature of the church, the meaning

of church membership, and the procedures and bases for membership acceptance, discipline, and removal. These documents need not be legal treatises; it is not necessary to list all the specific conditions under which the church's various forms of discipline may be exercised. The documents should set forth the basic expectations of members to live consistent with the calling of Scripture and discipleship.

2. *It may be expressed in formal church covenants.* Many churches, especially in Baptist traditions, have developed a specific church covenant that all members affirm as part of joining the church and that may be reaffirmed at various points in the church's life. The covenant commonly expresses a commitment to holy living in accord with Christ's call and may contain specific commitments both affirmative and negative (e.g., to support the church with tithes and offerings, to refrain from sexual immorality, to abstain from alcohol). While often such documents seem to express cultural judgments as much as they do biblical principles, they are, whatever their specific content, another important form of "notice" to the members of the expectations of membership. Further, they are specific agreements by the members, covenants they make with one another before God.

3. *It ought to be a regular part of church membership training.* As we have noted throughout, church discipline is not simply acts of expulsion, it is part of the entire discipling and nurturing ministry of the church. Church membership training is central to any larger, more biblical understanding of church discipline. It is also a key arena where "notice" is provided. In regard to the possibility of formal discipline by the church, potential members should be advised of the expecta-

tions of membership, the potential and practice of church discipline in the community, the understanding of its theological and biblical bases and purposes, and any procedures that the church follows.

4. *It should be a subject of preaching and teaching.* The church also gives notice to members by its teaching and preaching ministries. Are the expectations of membership part of the teaching ministry of the church? If the church understands Matthew 18 as governing the basic practice of church discipline, is it taught in the church? Are there courses that explain the church's central doctrinal commitments, its moral expectations, its procedures of discipline, the biblical rationale for particular church discipline practices?

5. *It ought to be practiced by the church.* A final important form of notice is the actual practice of the church. If the church practices church discipline in all its forms and in accord with its teachings and governing documents, that further makes all members aware that these formal provisions are in fact as well as in theory a part of the church's order. On the other hand, if it fails to practice what it preaches, members may legitimately be surprised when suddenly they are the targets.

The effect of these combined means of education or "notice" will be to provide both "implied" and "actual" notice in a legal sense and also to make spiritually and functionally clear to all what the church stands for and how it governs its life.

It is important both for purposes of assisting courts to understand the nature of church discipline and also for the edification of the church that church discipline be developed

AN ARTICULATED, THEOLOGICAL RATIONALE

on a sound biblical basis. Courts and church members need to understand that this is not simply a matter of an associational right or some novel notion of an authoritarian cult group. Rather, these principles are rooted in the religious faith of the community that practices them in obedience to Scripture and the Lord. They are exercises of a sincerely held religious belief and central to the community's understanding of its nature and calling.

The formal church documents, the membership training, and any acts of church discipline should be rooted in core biblical convictions and identified as such.

In a legal context, those carefully identified commitments will assist courts in understanding the dangers of judicial intrusion into this area of the church's life. Since it is a matter of essential doctrinal and religious practice, the courts should be on notice of the dangers of inhibiting such free exercise of religion or entangling themselves in the life of the church in this doctrinal area.

Developing a theological, biblical rationale may also help the church understand the nature and practice of church discipline and avoid an improper discipline based on unbiblical concepts and attitudes. Going through the exercise might provide a valuable insight into the meaning of the church in our day.

CONSISTENCY OF PRACTICE

Development of a carefully articulated rationale for church discipline that is duly communicated to the membership will not be sufficient. Again in both a spiritual and legal context it is important that there be a consistent practice of the discipline. This consistency has at least three aspects: first, a consistency in terms of actual implementation of the doctrinal commitments; second,

▶241

an evenhandedness in applying the principles; and third, a continuous concern for the values and principles that may occasion discipline and not a focusing on such values only at the point of formal censure or expulsion.

If the church shows patterns of inconsistency, discrimination, and uncertainty about applying its standards and principles, it ought not be surprised if a recipient of discipline calls "foul." James warns us of favoritism, "respect of persons," and partiality.[2] It is too easy to exercise discipline on the unpopular or the troublemakers and apply different standards to friends, the powerful, donors, and leaders.

As noted earlier, one basis for judicial interference occasionally is that the church, even though empowered to exercise church discipline including the expulsion of members, has not followed proper procedures. This involves not so much *what* the church did as *how* it did it.

PROPER PROCEDURES

WHAT ARE PROPER PROCEDURES? First, proper procedures are those already established by the church. The most important requirement is to follow carefully the written procedures set forth in the governing church documents, such as bylaws, covenants, or other formally recorded actions by the church. In the absence of specific written processes, the church's prior practices may constitute its unwritten but agreed upon and binding procedures.

Certainly there is no reason to become overwrought because a court expects a church to abide by its own rules. As we have

seen, courts will often intervene where associations, including religious groups, have not
granted to their members the procedural
rights they have "guaranteed" them in their
charters, bylaws, and previous practices.

These rules need not be extensive and detailed. In fact, overly defined and detailed
procedures may only invite persons who are
so inclined to search for flaws and use them
as a basis for dragging out the process either
in the church or in the courts. Such procedures ought, however, to include some basic
provisions that seem to embody fairness
principles, for example: right to notice of the
charges, right to a hearing before the body
that decides (elders or congregation), adequate notice of any meeting to be held including the time, place, and purpose of such
a meeting. It would hardly be "fair" to advise members of a meeting but not notify the
person involved that its purpose was to expel him or her.

Second, proper procedures may include
minimal standards of fairness (due process)
even if not required by church law or practice. As we noted earlier, in the absence of
any expressed procedures courts may impose some minimum standards of notice and
hearing. These ought not, however, become
a problem or the basis for lawsuits since
such requirements merely embody basic
principles of justice, and churches ought to
be eager to utilize procedures that embody
these rights.

Procedural properness does not mean the
church must become a highly technical forum like a court with specific and rigid rules
for trials, witnesses, evidence, etc. It does
mean that the church and its leadership
must have a reasonable procedure, know
what it is, and apply it.

It is self-evident that any information communicated in the process of church discipline be accurate and that it be communicated in good faith with a reasonable belief in its accuracy and with a proper motive. There are two important elements here: accuracy in fact and accuracy in implication.

ACCURACY AND GOOD FAITH

Accuracy or truthfulness is clearly a reasonable expectation both as a matter of law and because of the church's moral commitments. Absolute accuracy is sometimes difficult to achieve, and, as noted in the section on defamation, courts have normally granted a qualified privilege even for defamatory statements when in the context of proper investigation and implementation of church discipline. If the motive is proper (good faith), a reasonable belief in the accuracy of the facts may result in a qualified privilege even if the alleged facts later turn out to be inaccurate.

Certainly any report or announcement by church leaders to the church as a whole should be truthful in fact and in implication. There is something of a catch-22 here. The more accurate and complete the disclosure of facts, the more likely a disciplined member is to sense an invasion of privacy and to be legitimately embarrassed by the revelations.

In corrective church discipline, persons, ministries, and reputations are often at stake. Gossip and false charges are cruel weapons. Church leadership must be careful in dealing with charges against members and leaders. There are biblical principles that apply here, such as not entertaining charges against elders except where supported by other evidence, listening to both sides, rejoicing in good. In fact, church discipline may need to be exercised more often in rebuking gossips and rumormongers than in correcting wrongdoers.

Information must not only be accurate, but it must not be misleading. A charge that a person, Mary Smith, was suspended for "immoral conduct with John Johns" may be misleading if the issue was contractual fraud on a home repair job.

LIMITING THE "AUDIENCE" TO THE COMMUNITY OF INTEREST

The posture of the law here is in accord with common sense and/or biblical principles. The law arguably provides a limited or qualified privilege for disclosure of otherwise private information communicated within a legitimate community of interest but not the right to "blab it all over town." Only those with a legitimate interest, as discussed earlier, have this privilege.

TO WHOM MAY THE INFORMATION BE GIVEN? The scope of the audience will be determined by a number of factors, including the following: (1) the nature of the conduct, (2) the scope of present public knowledge, (3) the nature of the relationship of the one being disciplined to potential recipients of the information, (4) the nature of the relationship of potential recipients to the person or group communicating the information, and (5) the duties of the recipients of information.

Some of these factors go to the nature and scope of the acts for which the discipline is being administered. But other elements are also significant. The form of church government may be a factor since the church's structure may give specific responsibility to certain groups for such matters. In a congregational church, often the entire congregation would have final disciplinary authority, and hence they are proper recipients of a rather full disclosure in order to properly carry out their duties as members. If, on the other hand, disciplinary decisions are made by elders or deacons, then perhaps the information revealed to the whole congregation should be somewhat less detailed, informing them of the disciplinary action and instruction as to their responsibilities.

It certainly seems to us that in the normal situation, the disclosure and entire process is for the *church* and its members, not for outsiders. It is appropriate, therefore, for any discussion of issues of discipline to be confined to the members of the church, dismissing nonmembers from the meetings. This may argue for such matters being dealt with outside the Sunday morning worship context when there are often nonmembers in the service.

WHAT ABOUT DISCLOSURE TO OTHER CHURCHES? It is apparent that Miss Guinn did not approve of the notice given to the sister churches of the Collinsville Church of Christ. Yet certainly from a theological position, other churches, especially those with a relationship to the disciplining church, are part of the legitimate community of interest, and historically, churches shared such information. In any denominational tradition there is a mutual accountability. In some traditions, such as the Brethren, there were appeals from local church disciplinary decisions to a larger annual meeting. Today, of course, relationships between churches are often tenuous with relatively little mutuality of ministry or accountability. Among the factors that might determine whether there is a legitimate community of interest beyond the local church are the following: (1) proximity of the other churches, (2) degree of relationship between the churches, (3) scope of prior knowledge among members of other churches about the disciplined member generally and about the specific conduct at issue, (4) degree of any relationship of the disciplined party to the other congregations, and (5) specific need for the information by the other church, such as in the case of potential transfers of membership.

It would probably also be proper to distinguish between a general release of information to other churches and a response to a specific request for information in connection with, for example, employment or transfer of membership where the need for the information is much more evident.

RESTRICTING THE SCOPE OF INFORMATION DISCLOSED

The limited privilege available suggests, as does common sense, that what may be revealed also depends on the legitimate interests of the group to whom the information is being revealed. Therefore, it is appropriate for a church to limit the information to what is specifically relevant to the audience under the particular circumstances.

The information given to church leaders might appropriately be more detailed than that provided the general membership, especially if the decisions in such matters are primarily handled by a leadership group. The church should keep in mind the legitimate aspects of personal privacy. Church discipline is not an occasion for a sort of voyeurism.

It is not possible to supply specific formulas. We can only urge a careful assessment of the scope of the information to be revealed at each stage of the process, bearing in mind the duties or roles of the audience and the goal of assisting the church and its members in redemptive discipline.

In a general sense, what we are suggesting is that the church develop a responsible and well-grounded process for handling church discipline matters. This does not require rigidity, but the church will be in a position to avoid confusion and mere reaction when such issues arise.

PLANNING VERSUS REACTING

It behooves churches to review various areas of their ministry for potential problems in the areas noted in this volume, such as the counseling ministries, record keeping, and observing of formalities in all regular church business meetings. This may require the revision of church bylaws or adjustments in operating procedures. Again, such an effort ought not focus merely on reducing "exposure" in a legal sense but on conducting all the affairs of the church in a proper, biblically faithful, and consistent way.

Too often churches that rarely encounter a situation of discipline will be reactive, shaping their policies on emotional grounds or even on fear of lawsuits. Where churches believe they may be in a position that poses legal issues or problems, they would do well to consult legal counsel before the church is deeply enmeshed. But the church's sensitive and biblically rooted practices will be more important than lawyers.

---

[1]Chuck Colson, "Another Point of View: The Church Should Mind Its Own Business," *Jubilee,* April 1984, 3.

[2]James 2:1-13.

NOTES

APPENDICES

APPENDICES

1

THE BIBLICAL CHURCH DISCIPLINE PROCESS

The body of Christ is made up of forgiven men and women who still have a propensity to sin. Because we have been called out and predestined we are different, but we have not arrived at where we should be or desire to be. Until that time we will continue to be full of human weaknesses. As a result we need church discipline to maintain the purity of each individual saint and the body of Christ.

Church discipline in its broadest sense involves a continued growth process. Its aim is to present every man complete (mature) in Christ, not perfect.

THE PROCESS OF CHURCH DISCIPLINE

We cannot talk about church discipline without mentioning discipleship. Both words have the same root meaning. An emphasis on discipleship must and should precede any practice of church discipline. We must dedicate ourselves to being followers and imitators of Jesus Christ.

Romans 12:1, 2 tells us we are to be transformed, not conformed, to the world. Believers should be different from the world. Transformation is the mainspring to nonconformity. True nonconformity to the world, then, occurs only when there has been an experience of transformation. The Lord uses many means to transform us. One of those means is through individual and corporate church discipline.

In any discussion of church discipline the most frequently mentioned passage is Matthew 18:15-17. This passage deals with the larger picture of church discipline mentioned above. Two of the three times our Lord mentions the church in the Gospels are in this passage. This passage deals with church discipline in individual-to-individual relationships and in church-body-to-individual relationships. It includes several different aspects of activity and involvement.

SELF-EXAMINATION. The first aspect of church discipline involves self-examination. In 1 Corinthians, Paul tells the church at Corinth that there have been some dire consequences among church members because many have taken from the Lord's Table in an unworthy manner. In chapter 11:28, 29 he says, "But let a man examine himself, and so let him eat of the bread and drink of the cup. For he who eats and drinks, eats and drinks judgment to himself, if he does not judge the body rightly."

Paul also reminds us in Galatians 6:1, "Brethren, even if a man is caught in any trespass, you who are spiritual, restore such a one in a spirit of gentleness; each one looking to yourself, lest you too be tempted." To be involved in effective church discipline we must examine ourselves for sin and make sure we are not performing a righteous act in an unrighteous manner. In the Sermon on the Mount Jesus told us to take the beams out of our own eyes before we attempt to take the specks out of our brothers' eyes. Many times we will see as a result of going through this process that what we thought was a grievous sin on the part of our brother was, in fact, distorted by the obstruction (sin) that was in our own lives.

This self-examination should be ongoing and should produce men and women who partake of the Lord's Table in a worthy and proper manner, resulting in continued awareness of the required holiness of the saints. This self-examination will also produce the first needed step in any disciplinary process by assuring that those involved are doing it in the right spirit and not out of judgment.

GOING TO A BROTHER IN PRIVATE. The second aspect of church discipline involves the first step mentioned in Matthew 18:15. If our brother has sinned (missed the mark), then we are to go to him in private and reprove him. Several key ingredients are necessary in order to do this properly.

And if your brother . . .

This implies a relationship between the two individuals. For effective individual discipline apart from the corporate body there must be a relationship. The Psalmist David talked about the wounds of a faithful friend being better than the kisses of an enemy.

. . . sins . . .

What constitutes missing the mark? What sin is big enough to entail my response of going to my brother? Note that this is missing God's mark. It does not involve any action on the part of our brother that is not to our liking or according to our preference. On the individual basis the sin could be personal, directed at the person who is doing the confronting, or it could be some other known sin that has affected other people, other relationships, or brought dishonor to the Lord and his church.

. . . go . . .

This is a command and not an option. If our brother sins it is our personal responsibility to go just as much as it is our personal responsibility to go into all the world and proclaim the gospel. To not go is to disobey. Of course, when we go we go in the right spirit having followed step one mentioned above. How we go is just as important as obeying the command to go. Galatians 6:1 tells us to go in a spirit of gentleness with the purpose of restoring our brother, not judging him, lest we be tempted.

. . . and reprove him . . .

Our responsibility is to find out whether the offense named has been committed if we do not already personally know. In that instance we are fact finders. If it is revealed that an offense has been committed, then we deal with it.

If we are personally aware of the sin as we go, then we confront our brother in love. Our duty is to speak God's Word and make sure the individual sees that he has sinned and/or violated God's Word. In doing this we always distinguish between the person and his performance (i.e., God hates the sin but loves the sinner).

. . . in private. . . .

The purpose for this is obvious. It decreases someone's natural defensiveness and shows the highest regard for the individual and his privacy. Again the purpose for going is not to inflict judgment or punishment but to restore.

TAKING ONE OR TWO WITNESSES WITH YOU. The next part of dealing with the individual-to-individual discipline entails the second step of Matthew 18:16. The Scripture states that we are to again go to our brother in private with one or two witnesses. The logic of this is that hopefully the erring brother will see the seriousness of the transgression or dispute and seek to make things right. Also, the presence of the additional witnesses will serve to confirm that the action in question amounted to missing the mark and that refusing to repent from such action was a matter the church took seriously.

The Scriptures make it plain that this step comes only after the first attempt in private on a one-to-one basis has failed and after the brother has refused to listen. The procedure outlined allows several opportunities for the sinning brother to repent and be restored. In fact, the verb tense used in this passage implies a continual going. In other words, we go and continue to go to our brother in private until he refuses to listen to us or to meet to discuss the issue. At that point the two witnesses are brought along for the purpose of restoring the errant brother.

Of course, the attitude of all those going to the erring brother must be in accordance with the attitudes mentioned above.

DEALING WITH THE NONREPENTANT BROTHER. The final step in church discipline involves the action of the local church body. The charge is brought before the church, presumably by the offended brother and the two witnesses. The church offers an opportunity for the erring brother to repent and be restored. If he fails to repent, then according to Matthew 18 he is to be treated as a nonbeliever.

Churches interpret and apply this passage in many different ways regarding how a brother is removed and how he is to be treated. The action taken by a church can involve excommunication and shunning or, in cases involving less serious offenses, removal from office and/or refusing to allow participation in the observance of the Lord's Supper.

Whatever action the local church polity determines to be appropriate should certainly involve an attempt to show the church's love and acceptance of the sinner yet a rejection of the sin. If the brother wants to repent, he needs to know how to do it and how to be restored. Whatever the decision, the church's doors should remain open to all who truly repent.

What sins should receive the public discipline of the church?

According to the scriptural examples and models, the types of sins that should receive public discipline of the church include irresolvable disputes between members, persistent teaching of wrong doctrine (heresy), and continued immorality and/or contentiousness.

2 GUIDELINES AND PRACTICAL HELPS

What can prevent you from being sued? Nothing. Anyone with enough money to file a petition in a court can sue you no matter how frivolous the suit might be. There is no absolute way to ensure that you will not be sued. However, you can do some things right now to minimize the number of real and threatened lawsuits as well as the amount of damages that could be recovered as a result of church discipline. However, this chapter does not constitute legal advice. Your lawyer should be consulted in whatever action you or your church takes. The following guidelines spring out of common sense and fairness in response to the various legal issues and precedents present in discipline cases. Hopefully, they will help you as you seek to implement restorative church discipline.

PURCHASE INSURANCE. One alternative offered to churches and their leaders is some type of malpractice insurance. But one drawback to securing an insurance policy is that it actually invites lawsuits. Plaintiffs and their attorneys look for "deep pockets"—those that may have a lot of money.

There may be some deeper theological problems with securing secular insurance to pay the "debts" of one Christian to another. The purchase of insurance may indicate that a church does not feel 100 percent confident about its right to engage in church discipline or that its procedures are correct.

DO NOT CHANGE. If you are now in a church discipline action, do not change your procedures, constitution, or other courses of conduct unless they are totally inappropriate according to the other suggestions contained in this book. If you change anything, be sure that you follow your own steps and requirements scrupulously. Many times you may not need to change the form if you can change the substance by a turn in direction, purpose, or attitude of those administering the discipline.

BE PREPARED AHEAD OF TIME. Establish church discipline procedures before a discipline situation arises. If you currently have an informal process, formalize it. The following points will help you develop effective church discipline procedures:

1. Bring church members under the authority of Scripture regarding conduct and discipline (2 Tim. 3:16).

2. Make sure church members understand the scriptural purposes and procedures of church discipline. (Many churches use their church covenant to convey this understanding and secure their members' commitment.)

3. Each church leader charged with carrying out discipline must be qualified and beyond reproach. This is needed lest the leader be intimidated and respond by being too harsh or too weak.

4. The church must be committed to applying scriptural discipline consistently (regardless of the sin or the sinner).

5. The church should seek to have a well-rounded ministry with the members maturing in their faith.

6. The church must develop a system of discipline that is theologically sound within the confines of its doctrinal beliefs and its own polity.

The most common way to establish these procedures is to include them and their rationale in the articles of incorporation, charter, or bylaws of the church.

Churches must address two issues when adopting discipline procedures. These include obtaining the commitment of current members and informing new members of their rights and obligations when they join the church. The most obvious way is for church members to sign or agree to a covenant between each other relating to the topic and to secure the agreement of new members as they join.

GIVE NOTICE. Any theology of church discipline should provide for clear and timely notice to the unrepentant sinner.

ESTABLISH A THEOLOGICAL BASIS. The theological basis for church discipline (the rationale) should be in the same document (the articles of incorporation, charter, or bylaws) that includes instructions on the procedures and attitudes of those implementing the discipline.

PROVIDE TEACHING. We suggest that church leaders teach their congregations the principles of dispute resolution contained in Matthew 18; 5:23, 24; and 1 Corinthians 6:1-8. Encourage members to become peacemakers.

BE DISCREET. To whom should the sin be revealed or confessed? The logical answer consistent with the biblical pattern is that the sin be confessed only to those who know about it. If it is a publicly known sin, then the entire church should hear the confession. Otherwise, the circle of confession should not be any larger than those affected and those charged with helping restore the sinner.

In any public church disclosure of sin, the church needs to ensure that those hearing the report are within the "community of interest." This generally includes at least the adult members of the church. All visitors, permanent nonmembers, and suspended members should be requested to leave and if necessary escorted out of the meeting. The church may place any other restriction it desires upon those who will be in the meeting, such as including only those who have prayed for the unrepentant sinner.

DEAL WITH CURRENT MATTERS. One legal issue concerns the revealing of past acts that have no bearing on the present situation. We doubt that a church would seek to discipline someone for something they did five years ago, but we did want to mention it. The discipline process should be close in time to the sin in order to fully protect the privileged nature of the discipline and any disclosure.

It would be permissible to declare past offenses only in showing the habit pattern of an unrepentant sinner and to better inform the church of what it might take for the sinner to repent and be restored.

3 SAMPLE FORMS FOR USE IN CHURCH DISCIPLINE

THE CHURCH CONSTI- TUTION

The following article was taken from Article VI: Church Discipline, of the Constitution of the Trinity Baptist Church of Wheaton, Illinois.

SECTION 1. FORMATIVE DISCIPLINE.   God has ordained that through the comprehensive and faithful preaching of his Word the members of local churches be taught to walk so as to please him. The ministry of the church is to "Preach the word; be instant in season, out of season; reprove, rebuke, exhort with all longsuffering and doctrine" (2 Tim. 4:2). In addition to this, the church must build up its members by the use of the spiritual gifts of both young and old. If mutually sanctifying influences of the whole body, as taught in 1 Corinthians 12:12-27, be well understood, and every member be satisfied with his God-appointed place, we shall all "grow in grace, and in the knowledge of our Lord and Saviour Jesus Christ" (2 Pet. 3:18). We acknowledge that one's failure to respond properly to formative discipline leads to the necessity of implementing subsequent sections of this article.

SECTION 2. CORRECTIVE DISCIPLINE.
Corrective discipline is necessary because of conduct or doctrine contrary to biblical standards. No offenses shall be brought before the church until the instructions of the Lord Jesus Christ have been followed as outlined in Matthew 5:23, 24 and Matthew 18:15, 16. Corrective discipline always aims for the glory of God, the welfare and purity of the local church, and the restoration and spiritual growth of the offender.

(a) Suspension. There are occasions when a member's slackness in the performance of duty, disorderliness, and departure from the traditions and instructions of the Word of God require church discipline—but of a less severe nature than excommunication (see 2 Thess. 3:6, 11, 14-15). Nevertheless, serious offense may not be overlooked altogether lest God's enemies multiply their blasphemies, other saints be emboldened to sin, and the offender be harmed by a failure to test his own soul and appreciate the gravity of his offense. Therefore, if a member's disorderliness requires discipline, the church may suspend the offender from church membership and publicly rebuke him through the elders at a duly called congregational meeting. The congregation has the right and responsibility to suspend such a one by two-thirds majority of the members present and voting. This discipline consists of temporary suspension of rights to participate in the Lord's Table, to serve publicly in the church, and to vote in congregational meetings. The offender is not to be treated as an enemy but admonished as a brother.

(b) Excommunication. It is right and in harmony with the Scriptures for the congregation to exclude from the fellowship any member who persistently holds false and heretical doctrine, or is unwilling to settle differences in a scriptural manner, or openly and persistently lives inconsistently with his Christian profession, lives in violation of the law or public morals, or persistently disturbs the peace and unity of this church. This discipline may occur when suspension fails to secure the offender's repentance or may be enacted without prior corrective steps if the offense is of a sufficiently serious nature. First, written charges shall be filed with the eldership. Then, the accused shall have the right to present his own defense in person at a duly called congregational meeting. After a fair and impartial hearing of all the witnesses accessible and all the facts ascertainable, the congregation has the right and the responsibility to excommunicate an offending member by two-thirds majority of the members present and voting. If the accused is absent from the congregational meeting, a record of the proceedings shall be sent to him by mail. The church is required to deal subsequently with excommunicated individuals according to Matthew 18:17 and 1 Corinthians 5:1-13.

(c) Restoration. The church must restore to fellowship in full forgiveness those persons who show satisfactory evidence of repentance (2 Cor. 2:6-8). Persons shall be restored at a duly called congregational meeting upon recommendation of the elders and two-thirds majority of the members present and voting.

THE STAGES OF EXPULSION

THE CHARTER PROVISION. The purpose for which said corporation is formed is the worship of almighty God according to the faith, doctrine, discipline, and usages of the _____ church or denomination, by which all questions of faith, doctrine, and discipline shall be decided. Membership in said corporation shall be entirely subject to the rules, regulation, usages, canons, discipline, and requirements of said church or denomination, and a member expelled or suspended therefrom shall immediately cease to be a member of said corporation until fully restored to membership in good standing in said church or denomination.

The statutory and charter provisions upon which the above form is based were held sufficient to terminate membership in a religious corporation upon expulsion from the denomination with which it was connected (Merman v. St. Mary's Greek Catholic Church [1935] *317 Pa. 33*).

THE CHARGE. After careful investigation of the report, we the undersigned brethren of the _____ church at _____ deem it our duty to present a charge against Brother _____ for [here set forth accusation in detail including places and dates]. [Signatures.] (*Swafford v. Keaton* [1919] 23 Ga. App. 238.)

THE OFFICIAL RECOMMENDATION. We, the undersigned, elders of the _____ church at _____, having heard an evil report concerning Brother _____, to the effect that he had: [here insert detailed statement of accusation with places and dates], it being our duty to investigate the truth or falsity of said report, gave the whole matter a thorough examination, hearing all those whom we could expect to give us any evidence or facts concerning the matter. Having done this, we find the said report to be true

in the following respects: [here set forth in
detail with places and dates findings made
as a result of investigation]. In consequence
of the above findings, we are compelled to
pronounce Brother _____ a disorderly
member of the church and in accordance
with our rules of discipline to recommend his
expulsion from the same. [Signatures of the
elders.] (*Lucas v. Case* [1872, Ky.] 9 Bush
297.)

THE JUDGMENT AND SENTENCE. Whereas the
members of this church having entered into
a solemn covenant for the maintenance of
church discipline; and, whereas Brother
_____, unmindful of his covenant en-
gagement, has clearly violated the same in
that he has: [here set forth in detail with
places and dates the accusation proved
against the member], and thereby brought
dishonor on the name of him whom he has
avowed as his God and Savior, and grieved
the hearts of his brethren of this church, and
given occasion to the enemy to speak re-
proachfully; and, whereas he has been faith-
fully and patiently dealt with agreeably to
Christ's direction, and earnestly entreated
publicly to confess his offense, and thus remove the reproach resting on the cause of
Christ, and comfort the hearts that are aggrieved; and, whereas after much patient
waiting and affectionate expostulation by
the brethren, he declines publicly to acknowledge and deplore his offense, deliberately preferring expulsion from this church to
such an act of just humiliation; therefore, be
it resolved, first: that in deep sorrow of
heart, but in obedience to God's commands,
we separate Brother _____ from the
visible church of God, and no longer consider
him as having any claim on our communion
and fellowship. Resolved, second: that this

church does now as always bear its solemn testimony against the sin of [here insert appropriate description of ground upon which member is expelled] as an unfruitful work of darkness, eminently dishonorable to the God of purity and love [or other more appropriate description with relation to the ground of expulsion]; polluting to the soul of man and fearfully prejudicial to the welfare of society and of the world. Resolved, third: that if at any time Brother _____ shall give evidence of sincere repentance, and a disposition to return to God, and make his peace with him, it will give great joy to this church to open their arms and receive him to a participation in all their privileges, hopes, and consolations. As pastor of this church, and by their direction, I do now therefore publicly and solemnly declare the fellowship hitherto existing in holy things between Brother _____ and the visible church, to be, and it hereby is, dissolved.

The pastor of the expelling church was held privileged in reading to his congregation the judgment or sentence of expulsion upon which the above form was based (Farnsworth v. Storrs *[1850, Mass.] 5 Cush. 412.*)

THE NOTICE TO MEMBERS. To whom it may concern: This is to certify that on the _____ day of _____, 19__, fellowship was withdrawn from one _____, a member of the _____ church at this place. The charges against him were: [here set forth in detail charges upon which member was expelled], and therefore we cannot commend him as worthy of the confidence of the brotherhood. Any other information that is wanted will be given upon request. [signatures.]

The notice upon which the above form was based as published in the denominational journals was held to be a privileged communication in a libel action (Redgate v. Rousch [1900] 61 Kan. 480).

NOTE: The forms above were taken from 20 A.L.R.2d, 520-522.

A SAMPLE PUBLIC ANNOUNCEMENT

It has come to the attention of the board that a member of our church must be dealt with by church discipline. The church board has carefully and thoroughly investigated the facts and has confirmed that discipline is necessary. The parents and the Board have appealed to the one who has sinned. All attempts have so far been rejected. Scripture now instructs us to inform the church so that the united prayer and obedience of the members to the scriptural steps of discipline may be used of God to bring this person to repentance and to a life of victory over sin. Before naming this person we are asking each member to set aside a time of personal self-examination, confession of sin, and commitment to God's instructions of church discipline and restoration. We are doing this so that Satan will be given no opportunity to bring confusion or division in this matter and that God may be free, because of our obedience, to accomplish his purposes in the life of the one who has sinned.

4 COUNTING THE COST

In the preceding sections we saw that there is no way to prevent churches from being sued. But they can by their actions minimize any damages as well as discourage frivolous lawsuits from being filed. Any lawyer will admit that bad facts make bad law. If a church exercises discipline without either recognizing or caring about the important issues within the legal arena that affect its right to exercise that discipline, then it is a sitting duck: It may well become a precedent-setting case, and a bad one at that.

The church that seeks to minister biblical discipline can be assured of two things. First, the tide of sentiment among the general public and in many Christian circles mitigates against the faithful practice of that discipline. Some of the most vociferous attacks may come from the part of the Christian community that feels threatened or convicted by the practice of biblical discipline.

The world's reaction is understandable because it operates only in the physical world, whereas churches operate in both the physical and spiritual reality. Thus churches should anticipate challenges.

The second thing churches can be assured of is that God is still on his throne. He is sovereign. He is in control. Even though the tide of sentiment may be flowing against the church, it is comforting to know that the Lord is not surprised or overwhelmed by this opposition.

In 1984 a family in Colorado was disciplined by their church (the First Baptist Church of Pagosa Springs). Outraged at being disciplined and put out of the church (mainly on the grounds of being contentious), all four family members instituted a lawsuit against the church seeking damages for defamation, intentional infliction of emotional distress, and invasion of privacy. They even asked that the court give them the church property. The lawsuit was filed in July. In late October all four family members were killed in an airplane crash while on an outing. The father, an experienced pilot, got lost in bad weather and crashed into the eastern slope of the Rocky Mountains.

While this true story sounds almost like the story of Ananias and Sapphira of the New Testament, it is not intended for pastors to use as a tool to threaten members who pose potential discipline problems. We share the story to remind us all of the reality of the spiritual world. Anyone involved in corrective biblical discipline is involved in spiritual conflict. To be good soldiers of the Cross we must not only equip ourselves with the armor of God mentioned in Ephesians 6, but we must do as Peter instructed: be sober in spirit, gird our minds for action, and fix our hope completely on the Lord Jesus Christ (1 Pet. 1:13).

As we remember from several passages in the Old Testament, God is interested in our obedience more than our sacrifices. Our obedience to him and his Word opens the door to presenting a more acceptable sacrifice. If the Lord leads your church or organization to implement biblical discipline, then you need to obey even though it is never easy or comfortable.

The purpose of these appendices is not to convince you to exercise biblical discipline but to equip you with the best possible tools to implement that discipline within our present legal system. We cannot urge you enough to follow the steps mentioned in the guidelines. These should minimize your legal risks as well as keep you consistent with the scriptural models for restoring a brother or sister in Christ.